# THE GIFT CALLED
# JESUS CHRIST

*Osmond Henry Owusu*

Bloomington, IN   Milton Keynes, UK
authorHOUSE

*AuthorHouse™*
*1663 Liberty Drive, Suite 200*
*Bloomington, IN 47403*
*www.authorhouse.com*
*Phone: 1-800-839-8640*

*AuthorHouse™ UK Ltd.*
*500 Avebury Boulevard*
*Central Milton Keynes, MK9 2BE*
*www.authorhouse.co.uk*
*Phone: 08001974150*

*First published by AuthorHouse 4/3/2006*

*ISBN: 1-4259-1127-7 (sc)*

*Printed in the United States of America*
*Bloomington, Indiana*

*This book is printed on acid-free paper.*

*The Author would like to acknowledge the publishers of the Webster's English dictionary and the Authorized King James Version of the Holy Bible. All Bible quotations are from the King James Version of the Holy Bible.*

# <u>DEDICATION</u>

This book is dedicated to the memory of my Late father Isaac Owusu, my beloved wife Felicia, and children: Theresa, Fred, Philip and Gideon. It is also dedicated to all people who are bent on pleasing the Lord Jesus Christ.

# APPRECIATION

What may be the best way of saying thank you to so many persons who have in one way or the other made this book a reality?

Let me thank the following:

1. The Holy Spirit for His inspiration, revelations, and enablement

2. Rev. Anane Asane and Rev. Dr. J. B. Ghartey for the herculean editorial and vetting work they did on the manuscripts

3. Rev. John Felix Yeboah, Rev. J. K. Sam, Rev. Wiredu Nkrumah, Rev. George Boaheng, and Rev. Steve Wengam for their fatherly or brotherly upbringing, counsel and encouragement

4. My lovely wife Felicia and children for their patience and unflinching support

5. Christian friends at Apam Secondary School who are Richard and Juanita Opuku, Ebo and Ellen Mbeah, Essah Amoaful and spouse Comfort, Philo Dagadu, Francis Asare, and Albert Benyarko for their support and encouragement.

# CONTENTS

# FOREWORD
# BY REV. WILLIAM W. DONTOH

**(GENERAL SUPERINTENDENT, ASSEMBLIES OF GOD, GHANA)**

This book has been written at a timely moment when many indeed lack the true knowledge of the person of Jesus Christ.

The times which we are is comparable to the event that occurred at Caesarea Philippi in Matthew 16 when Jesus asked His disciples who men and they thought He was. It was clear from the answers given that the public including the disciples of Jesus lacked the true revelation of who Jesus was. It took divine revelation imparted to Peter to reveal who Jesus was to the disciple.

Bro. Osmond, a prolific writer and a matured believer in Christ inspired by the Holy Spirit has revealed in this book Jesus as a gift to humankind, His deity and attributes as Governor, Counselor, Mighty God as stated in Isaiah 9:6. He reminds believers that Jesus as a gift must be received and the recipient must grow in His knowledge and operate by His operational principles. It is at this point that the gift will be of full benefit to the recipient.

Understanding the role and attributes of Jesus as Governor, Wonderful, Counselor, Mighty God, Everlasting Father and Prince of peace will enrich one's Christian life and equip the believer to access the benefits that go with His person.

Another fascinating revelation expounded by Bro. Osmond is the fact that the increase of His government shall know no end. This means that anyone associated with Him and submitting to His Lordship will experience limitless favor and blessings.

The message in this book has been made so simple and presented in a manner that one can use it as a Bible study guide.

I recommend this book for Bible schools and Ministers of the gospel who will want to teach their flock extensively on Christ. In fact, this book should be a must for every believer.

I wish to commend the author for this great work well done and pray it will bless people as it has done to me.

# INTRODUCTION

Some people picture Jesus Christ as a baby in a manger who is remembered around Christmas time. Others also see Him as a great teacher who once lived in the land of Palestine. Yet others see Him as a prophet who once lived. Some see Him as someone called the Savior, but not sure what He saves people from. Some argue He was black, others claim He was white. Many for His words and unending influence in the world have admired him. Some remember him only at Easters. He is mentioned in almost all the religions today, from an argumentative referential point anyway.

The crust of the matter is that His person, real mission, and purpose for coming to this world are often ignored. But this person called Jesus must be looked at again, in the light of scripture. One cannot ignore this person whose spiritual movement, at the human level is the most populous and powerful on the planet earth. Secondly, you cannot ignore Him for the miracles and life-changing effect through His Name and Word.

This treatise is designed to throw more light on the personage of Christ, what He came into the world to do, His thoughts towards you, and what He is capable of doing for anyone who decides to give Him the chance in his or her life. ***It is an expose on Isaiah 9: 6,7.***

In our key golden text, Isaiah 9: 6-7, the Bible echoes thus, *"For unto us a child is born, unto us a son is given: and the government shall be upon his shoulder: and his name shall be called Wonderful, Counselor, The Mighty God, The everlasting Father, The Prince of Peace. Of the increase of his government and peace there shall be no end, upon the throne of David, and upon his kingdom, to order it, and to establish it with judgment and with justice from henceforth-even forever. The zeal of the LORD of hosts will perform this."* We see in this golden text, a glimpse of the personage called Jesus Christ. The Holy Scripture is setting forth some key revelations about Him that must not be overlooked because they could change your life for your own good. These are keys to spiritual knowledge, which God revealed through His prophet Isaiah, showing who Jesus Christ really is, His purpose and mission on earth for you and me.

The text is showing Jesus Christ as a gift from God, the reason for His giving, His nature and what He can do. It also shows His attitude and strength for work, and lastly the eminent result of His working.

This treatise is therefore written as an attempt to let the reader see Jesus Christ in the light of scripture, and what He is capable of doing in one's life if He is given the slightest chance. It challenges our awareness as to what we may be missing without Christ; the extent to which we allow Him directly influence our success rate in life from God's viewpoint.

The reader is therefore challenged to humbly read this book prayerfully, and the Lord Jesus Christ will speak to him or her about Himself and what He is prepared to do in your life.

Some people may have the notion that they are just fine in this life by virtue of their possessions. These people are encouraged to accept the fact of truth that the life of a person (success) is not in the abundance of things he or she has (Luke 12: 15). It is the desire and prayer of the writer that the reader will realize that God desires to give him/her peace and an expected end (Jer. 29: 11). You are therefore urged by the mercies of Jehovah to read on, and read on, for you will encounter God.

This Gift of God is given by grace to us for our restoration. We lost all that we originally had from the Lord; and through this gift called Jesus Christ God is restoring as many as are willing unto our position of dignity and dominion. God is showing forth His righteousness in the Person called Jesus Christ. So that you and I could reign in this life to the very glory of Jehovah.

Rom 5: 15, 17 say, *"But the free gift is not like the offense. For if by the one man's offense many died, much more the grace of God and **the gift by the grace of one Man, Jesus Christ, abounded to many**. For if* *by the one man's offense death reigned through the one, much more **those*** ***who receive abundance of grace and of the gift of righteousness <u>will</u>*** ***<u>reign in life</u> through the One, Jesus Christ.***"

If you desire, in reality, to reign in this life then the good news is that, Christ came as the gift of the righteousness of God so that we could reign in every area of our life, through Him.

# CHAPTER ONE
# A GIFT

*'Your very attitude towards Christ Jesus determines what you could make out of Him,'*

OSMOND

## DEFINITIONS AND CONDITIONS OF A GIFT

From the golden text in Isaiah 9: 6a, *"For unto us a child is born, unto us a son is given...,"* the Bible emphatically states the circumstances under which Jesus Christ came to this world. Here, the Word of God indicates that Jesus Christ is a **Gift** given unto humanity. Thus, He was sent to us as a Gift from God the Father. As revealed in the text, there are some specific reasons for which Jesus Christ is given for our good and well-being.

Let us look at what a gift really is, the conditions attached to it, and its potency. A gift is something given out to other people or things we receive from people. Since payments we make for items bought all constitute something given what then is a gift? **A gift could then be defined, in simple terms, as something given out or received from someone not on the terms of debt or score settling (in negative sense).** Thus there must be no strings attached to it. When the item

1

is given to influence judgment or negatively influencea right course of action, then it becomes a bribe. A gift in its fullest sense is affirmed when it is received.

Thus it implies that Jesus Christ is given out to us with no strings attached. He is given to us not as a debt-settling object; in other words God does not owe us and is using Jesus Christ to pay us. But rather, He God is offering Christ to us as a token of His love for us. There is therefore no ulterior motive for God giving us Christ. **Jesus is then *the parcel of blessing* from the almighty God to us, a package of all the goodies of God to YOU! You must accept Him. Never miss this PARCEL.** *"And you are complete in Him..." Col 2: 10.*

## POTENCY OF THE GIFT

Every gift has the potency of being a blessing or otherwise to the recipient. The gift when received by someone becomes a seed in the person's life. The potential of that seed, in the gift, will be realized if the gift is put to its proper use. Thus a person could receive a gift and let it remain dormant; not put to use and therefore not realizing what the gift could do to him or her.

Therefore for any gift to be a blessing to you, you must first receive it; be able to know what it is made up of or what use one can put it; and then practically making use of it. A miss at any of these steps, by ignorance, presumption or whatever the reason could be, will cost you the full realization of the blessings that Gift is supposed to impact to your life.

Jesus Christ, by the Holy Scriptures, is given to us by God Jehovah as a Gift for our good. If any person desires to have the fullness of the blessings obtainable, then the person must go by the following steps. If that is your prayer, then you must:

- Receive Him. John 1: 12

- Grow in the knowledge of Him. 2 Pet 3: 18, Col 2: 2-3.

- Go by His operational principles (practically use gift as it is supposed to be used). John 15: 7, 16.

You may have realized by now that your very attitude towards Christ Jesus determines what you could make out of Him. Many people in the world today are rejecting Him, ALAS, to their own detriment. I strongly recommend Him to you today.

The scriptures reveal Jesus. Refuse to remain a spiritual baby for good, you need to grow up into a matured person. **Jesus Desires That You Know Him The More.**

It is not just enough knowing what Jesus is and what He says. When we are able to discover what a gift is, we must put the gift to use if the gift is designed to work. Imagine you are given a blender and

3

you want to use it to powder stones, obviously it will not work for you. Why, because you are not using it to do what it is designed to do? In the same way, if you decide to go outside the operational principles of The Lord Jesus Christ, things will not work for you. You follow what He says, you obey what He commands and that's it. If you do not want to do what He says, then forget it. You are responsible for every bit of the word of God you know. John 14: 21-24, 13-15.

You may have realized by now that many of us are in the church house today, and are still going through serious hustles and unrest in life because we haven't come to grips with what we have. We do not really know who Jesus Christ is, and how we can have His fullness of blessings.

Pause for a moment. Reflect on what you have read so far. If you have not given your life to the Lord Jesus truly, you better do so now. Maybe you have given your life to him but you are lazy at seeking him or even seriously learning of him. Maybe you are trying to live your life by your own standards and ways. Please you must repent of all these. Go before the LORD now in prayer. It is safer to be sincere before the God who knows all about us and also has the power to help us. The Bible says that Jesus Christ is able to save to the uttermost all that come to God through Him (Heb. 7:25).

# CHAPTER TWO
# GIFT FROM A BEING CALLED GOD

*'Jesus Christ is the Best ever that the Unique God Jehovah
has for humanity'*

*'Any experience of a person that may be held, as truth but
is contrary to the Bible is apparent knowledge and or a
straightforward lie. The Reality is Christ Jesus.'*

OSMOND

## THE UNIQUENESS OF GOD

We want to look at the Being called God, and relate Him to His
gift. The Being called JEHOVAH GOD is unique. He has no equal
to compete with Him. His attributes and characteristics make Him
outstanding. These qualities position Him far above all things and in
all realms of existence. As the philosopher said, He is the uncaused
Cause. He is before all things and all things were made by Him and
for Him. By His power the created order is sustained to operate the way
He fashioned them to, till this day. Indeed God is great and powerful.
Thus you and I, beasts of the field, fowls in the air, demons, angels;
things visible and invisible are all created and kept to operate as they
were made by him. He is the Creator, who Himself is uncreated (John
1: 1, Col 1: 15-18).

5

There are five essential attributes of God (qualities that make Him God). These attributes distinguish Him from every other being, and places God as God, unique, from every sense of the word. According to Dennis J. Mock in his book 'Bible Doctrine Survey,' God is:

- Spirit (Not physical, invisible, cannot be accurately represented by anything). (John 4: 23-34, Rom 1: 18-25).

We could thus imply that it is a total misguidance and folly to set up an idol for worship (Rom 1: 21-25). We really ridicule God when we involve ourselves in image worshipping of any form or kind (Exodus 20: 4-5).

- Life (Life is inherent in God; all life is sourced in and derived from God; He is the giver, sustainer, and taker of all life) (Col 1: 17, Gen 2: 7, John 1: 3-4).

We owe our very existence to God. All created things exist and function by God's power; our power of being is sourced in God. Thus He alone possesses the permit of existence for anyone or anything. All the arrogant, persons who are destitute of virtue, and the rebellious against God, exist just by His mercy (visible and invisible persons alike). We are accountable, concerning what we used life for, to Him who gave us the permission to live. We ought to show our gratitude to Him.

- Perfect (Totally flawless, exists in the state of absolute excellence, completely correct and accurate, complete, lacks nothing). (Matt 5: 48, Deut 32: 4, 2 Sam 22: 31).

God can never make a mistake in anything. God's principles and patterns for us are just the best for us. God's will, which is for our own safety, must never be denied. Supreme importance of the Word of God (the Bible) cannot be overemphasized here. God has the capacity to do **whatever** He desires to do to the letter; He does not lack anything for any purpose.

- Unique (Peerless and matchless, there is no one like Him; above creation). (2 Sam 7: 22, Isaiah 40: 10, Dan 4: 34-35).

No other being possesses the qualities of God and to the same extent. No other being deserves to be worshipped; there is no other God but the LORD. Whatever goodly qualities we may find in any being are simply what He God possesses and has imparted a little into that being. Think of some people who see themselves to be full of knowledge to the point that they ridicule God with what they term science, technology, reality and philosophy. **No other being can ever match God in anything.**

- Eternal (Is now, always has been and will forever be. No beginning and no end). (Ps 90: 2, 1 Tim 6: 16, Ex 3: 14, Is 40:13-14).

God is ageless: ever the same, qualities of being not abating nor diminishing with the passage of time. God created time. The framework of time then rests with God.

All that could happen within the realm of time ultimately will conform to the grand design of God who created the time. God has always existed, and shall always exist with the same qualities.

There are other qualities about God worth noting (**derived attributes from the essential ones**), for the purpose of our study. God is:

- Holy (Perfectly pure and permanently free from sin; He cannot sin). (1 Sam 2: 2).

God cannot sin. By virtue of His perfect purity, sin then becomes missing the standard set by God. Any action, thought or gesture that violates God's nature then is sin. God's central character is holiness that He proves to persons who get close to Him. You then have no choice but to be holy as well; thus without it you cannot then see God.

- Transcendent (Higher than and above all things). (Job 11: 7-8).

By virtue of His position as the Creator, God is above the totality of the created order. Any quality seen in God is astronomically, incomparably and infinitely far above and higher than in any other being. Thus instruction, knowledge, and wisdom of God are far higher than that of any other person. The logical obvious reasonable choice for knowledge and wisdom that grants real peace, safety, joy, success and wealth is that from God. The best then for everyone is to submit to the Lordship and Leadership of Christ.

- Self-existent (Ever living without the support of anything or anyone). (Isaiah 40: 13-14).

Only God exists without the support of anything. All other things, visible and invisible, depend on God for all things for life and existence. Physical life on earth resort to other physical things for survival (air, water, food from other living things), clothing (from other things), shelter, services, etc. The best support in all things then comes from the Lord. We need then to appreciate and yield our lives to the Lord Jesus Christ.

- Infinite (Has no limit in all His qualities and abilities; free from all limitations). (1 Ki 8: 27, Jer 23: 23-24).

God has no limit in any of His qualities. God cannot be worn down, in any of His capabilities, as He keeps things he has made in functional order. God cannot break down.

God is fully awake and conscious at all times. God is never short of any resource to do anything. Nothing can get out of His hand in this realm of existence.

- Immutable (Does not change for better or for worse).(Heb 13: 8).

God does not grow old or young. God does not increase or decrease in knowledge or experience. God does not change in His character of being nor does He change in the extent to which He could manifest a certain quality or ability of His nature. God does not change in His operational principles; they always conform to His nature. If God is to change, then He cannot be trusted for anything as God.

- Omnipotent (Possess all power, ability, and strength). (Jer 32: 17).

Any capacity to do something is sourced in God. Since everything else is created by God, the sum total of all power (spiritual and physical) in the created order (universe) emanated from God as well. Thus the total power in the whole universe is fractional of God's power.

God's omnipotence is also seen as the whole universe is kept in functional order. Everything humans came to realize in the universe is working as it has being programmed to. (Heb 1:1-3, Col 1: 16). His omnipotence is able to keep everything He has made under His ultimate control. Rev 21:1-10; thus nothing could get out of His control

- Omniscient (Knows and understands all things at all times). (Isaiah 46: 10).

All acts, facts and skills or anything called information that could ever be known, is known by God at all times. God possesses the requisite knowledge base needed for creation, sustenance of creation and beyond. God is the 'Intelligence' behind this complex systems or worlds of existence, visible and invisible, micro and macro levels called the universe. God possesses all wisdom, knowledge and skill to manage the universe to His desired end. God's will and principles for life are then the best. God possesses the knowledge of whatever things that are yet to happen tomorrow, today. Nothing takes God by surprise. God understands all things. Nothing is mysterious or complex for God to handle.

- Omnipresent (Everything is in His presence at all times). (Ps 139: 7-12).

All things God has made are in His presence at all times.

Nothing is secret before God. Because of His absolute responsibility over His creation, everything is manifest in His sight always. God is the faithful witness to every event in the universe. Nothing could ever be hidden in His sight. God then is the Just Judge over every case. Judgment will then be interesting. You can run but you can never hide.

- Sovereign (Possesses the right, authority and power to rule over and control all things according to His plan and will). (Is 46: 8-10).

The final and the ultimate right and authority to control anything is with God. The sovereignty of God is due to the fact that He is the Creator and Sustainer of the universe. God is then the King of Kings and Master of all lords. He is the final Authority. Every form of rule or authority that is not sourced in Him will be ultimately crushed (Heb. 12:25-28). Every other form of authority must then be subject to His sovereignty. God is accountable to none but Himself. His will is then the ultimate.

- Faithful (He always keeps His promise, and His actions and attitudes are consistent with His character). (2 Tim 2: 13).

God is fully and totally committed to whatever He stands for. God fully keeps His part of the deal to maintain a covenant with any person; whatever it takes for the relationship to stand. He will fulfill His obligations. God is totally responsible (could always be trusted to do the right and most sensible thing). God is truthful. God is trustworthy. God is always supportive for the right cause.

There are other qualities or attributes of God, which are **relational** in nature. They show how He relates to His creation. God is:

- Love (Voluntary commitment to seek the highest good of others always). (1 John 4: 8-11).

The central element of His nature is love. God is deeply caring. He is bent on seeing the total well being of others no-matter the cost; even the life of His Son Jesus. God bears long with us. God in His love hates sin, because sin destroys people

- Light (He reveals His true nature, salvation and absolute holiness). (1 Tim 6: 16, 1 John 1: 5).

God is the One who reveals truth or the reality of things in this life. God as light grants understanding into the essence of issues of life on earth and beyond the grave. God as light causes humans to come by and discover the very interstices and intricacies of their animate and inanimate environment, which He has made. God as light reveals His very nature and being to those who come near Him. God as light expels all forms of darkness everywhere He is functionally operative.

- Truth (Everything God is, says and does conforms perfectly to ultimate reality). (John 14: 6, Is 45: 19).

God as truth is the very embodiment of all factual knowledge, not the apparent but the very reality of knowledge (<u>what is really there to be known</u>). God as truth communicates and does only the reality; everything He is about is eternally enduring. Thus whatever He says is what really is and what to take place; you better believe the bible. <u>Any experience of man that may be held as truth, but is contrary to the Bible may be apparent knowledge and or a straightforward lie</u>. What we call truth is then enduring, trustworthy, constructive (positive sense), just as God is.

- Good (Always acts for the right motive seeking to accomplish that result which is beneficial, profitable, useful, and appropriate from His View). (Ps 34: 8).

Whatever God does is with the purest motive. We could trust in God, for His actions towards us are for our own benefit. All creatures in the universe stand to benefit from God's benevolence if they are reconciled to Him. By His goodness He could withhold from us anything we could pray for but may not be beneficial to us at that time.

- Wise (He alone understands all things and knows how to skillfully, perfectly and appropriately apply that knowledge to life to accomplish the desired results). (Dan 2: 20-21).

God is the best person to handle any situation. God alone knows the best way or the alternative to deal with any issue pertaining to life. We should rely on God for directions in life that is to yield the optimum results. It is unwise, then, to ignore God in any issue of life. No situation is difficult for Him. For all answers to every question in life, GO TO HIM. The closer we get to God the wiser we become.

- Just (He deals equitably with all persons by holding them accountable to Himself and to the same standard, while rewarding the righteous and punishing the wicked). (Jer 9: 24).

God's justice demands that all sin must be punished. His justice demands that all righteousness must be rewarded. God's standards of assessment, for either sin or holiness, cannot change (2 Tim 2:19). The wicked cannot go unpunished. Any response of God towards anyone is the fairest of treatments. God dispenses justice irrespective of the persons involved (no partiality).

- Merciful (Compassionately withholding what we deserve, punishment, for sin). (Ps 25: 6-7).

God shows pity to those who deserve punishment for the wrong things they do. Looking at all the wrong and sinful behaviors we put up, we are not consumed just by His mercy. The mercy of God must be appreciated and seen as a second chance to us to do what is right in His sight. As non-perfect humans, who deserve to be punished, the mercy of God grants us grace and blessings.

- Gracious (Freely giving to us what we do not rightly deserve, purposed to lift us to where He wants us to be). (Ps 111: 4).

By His gracious nature he makes available to us what we really need, so that our lives could bring glory to Him. What we could never have being able to get, His grace provides to us free of charge. By His grace we get what we do not rightly deserve. By His grace flows to us the necessary empowerment to enable us reach where He has purposed us to be. Any accomplishment of man that is to bring glory to God is through His grace. We can go through any situation and come out victorious by this same grace

- Wrath/Fire (His righteous anger and displeasure at and against sin and wicked persons; deep and intense repugnance and hostility towards anything called evil). (Rom 1: 18, Heb 12:29).

God cannot look at sin and be happy or indifferent. God exhibits an intense hostility towards all that we call sin and evil. God shows great annoyance towards all wicked persons. God makes sure the doer receives full consequence for an evil deed.

- Forgiving (Not holding us responsible for sin because Jesus paid the penalty for it). (Dan 9: 9, Eph 1: 7).

God lets go of His resentment towards us because someone (Jesus) has stood in to receive the punishment on our behalf. Rev 19:15b. Fellowship is restored between God and us because the hostility towards us, by the sin we committed, is removed. All the 'goodies' He has for man could be received because of the union through forgiveness. This forgiveness establishes peace with God and withing oneself.

- Patient (Self-restraint to punish sin because of His desire for men to repent and be saved). (1 Pet 3: 20).

God never wants us to go through the painful experience we go through by His discipline, but rather would wait if we could change for the better. For the benefit of doubt, he gives room for us to change, but if the change does not come , He then goes ahead to discipline us (Heb. 12:6-9). God desires strongly that we should repent, live in holiness and enjoy His blessings.

- Righteous (He is always right and always act in perfect accord to His holy character). (Ps 11: 7).

God sets the rules for the game; he determines what is right or wrong. God always will do things, which perfectly satisfies the very standards He has set. Whatever God does is always right. God cannot be wrong in any anything or in any way. By our limited understanding, we may not appreciate some of His principles and methods, but we discover their truthfulness when we grow.

These characteristics of God make Him just **unique.** He has no equal. WOW! God is really great and good.

## God's Gift Is Also Unique

From the perspective of seeing the worth of the gift, we first have to look at the state of being of the giver who is God. We cannot as rational beings fail to appreciate, admire, and in fact submit to the truth that God is indeed God. The characteristics of being of God discussed above go to prove that He possesses all right, power, and the capacity to do all that He wants to do. 'In Him we live and move and have our being' (Acts 17:28).

His relational qualities are simply what must even cause every person to accept God. He is loving, merciful, gracious, forgiving, patient etc. Therefore if this person has any gift to give, then it must also be unique. Pause and think about this very well. Based on who He is, what do you think are His thoughts and heart-felt desires concerning you? Beloved, you and I can't miss this for any reason. We must not allow ourselves to be deceived by anyone. Based on His nature, He has purposed a gift for mankind, from eternity past, which is meant to impact your life to His desired end; which in fact is weightier and far glorious than what we earthlings think we could ever have. **This gift of God, Jesus Christ, is therefore unique.**

## THE CONDITIONS AND POTENCY OF THIS GIFT

Whatever the gift is capable of doing in one's life when truly received is as what God designed it to do. But what it could possibly do in your life as you receive it depends on what you discover about it and the extent to which you cooperate with it. The other issue has to do with you even accepting and receiving this gift of God.

As Jesus told the Samaritan woman at the well in John 4:10, *'Jesus answered and said unto her,* **If thou knowest the gift of God,** *and who is it that saith to thee, Give me to drink…'.* If we really know this Jesus, the gift of God, as He Himself referred Himself to the woman, all our troubles should have being under control.

The crust of the matter is that Jesus Christ is more than capable of doing whatever the scriptures say He is given to us to do. People refuse Him thinking they are just okay in life, with some good paid jobs, a few cars, a home, some estate or property of a sort, some half-baked marriage riddled with quarrels, built a large hall for church services, etc. But a close examination of one's personal inner life reveals a serious shortfall to the standards of Jehovah. All have sinned and fallen short of the glory of God (Rom 3: 23).

All the things we can even boast of in life are not properly established and sustained; we sometimes even fear other people may rob us of them. With all the so-called modernity and technological advancement of mankind, the society is pitifully embattled with serious problems in all spheres of life. This is a clear indication of our need of the ultimate leadership and guidance of the Creator who is all wise, all-powerful, all knowing, etc. This greatly needed leadership and guidance is what the Lord God has parceled in the gift-package called Jesus Christ. Note that the ultimate level one could reach, where this gift could be laid aside is to be at par with Christ (Eph 4: 13). **Beloved we need God everyday.** Wherever you think you're, once you are not up to the level of Christ, you need this gift seriously. Whether in the Christian ministry, academics, business, politics, whatever, please humble yourself and consider God.

If we look at what God is made of, the manifestation of His invisible power in creation, one cannot doubt the ability of God to perform what He has said He would do. Secondly, God cannot lie. The Bible says He is not a man that He should lie, neither the son of man that He should repent. Thirdly, God is faithful. So you better believe what He says His gift is designed to accomplish in the life of people.

Once again, in Isaiah 9: 6-7, the marvelous text thunders, (*"For unto us a child is born, unto us a son is given: and the government shall be upon his shoulder: and his name shall be called Wonderful, Counselor, The Mighty God, The everlasting Father, The Prince of Peace. Of the increase of his government and peace there shall be no end, upon the throne of David, and upon his kingdom, to order it, and to establish it with judgment and with justice from henceforth-even forever. The zeal of the LORD of hosts will perform this").* The gift possesses the ultimate capacity of leadership and governance, works of wonder, counsel and direction, demonstration of the power of God, exercise of fatherhood responsibilities for good, and peace establishment. The text also reveals that when He is given the chance, the extent to which He could go is infinite. Also whatever He does is fully backed by the very strength and working ability of Jehovah God.

When Jesus met the Samaritan woman at the Jacob's well, and as He has met you today, ' ***If you knew the gift of God***, *and who it is who says to you, " Give me your heart," you would have asked Him, and He would have given you living water.* The woman was ignorant of who Jesus Christ was, and what He could possibly do for her. So do some of us. She did not know the gift of God for mankind; who was in the very person of Jesus Christ she was talking to. She did not know that the Thirst Quencher and Life Satisfier was the gift of God she was talking to. She was ignorant of the truth that Jesus is come to bring life in place of all the deadness in every area of our lives. **He is still giving the water of life freely, my dear reader.** If you examine your life carefully, is this all that you could possibly become? **We still need Jesus Christ.**

You know, its prayer time! Lets get to God in prayer; pour your heart before Him because He cares for you. Tell Him about what you have learnt about His gift so far and what you desire to receive from this gift.

# CHAPTER THREE
# THE GOVERNOR

*'All proper governance for a life or society to produce peace
and security rests on the shoulders of Jesus Christ (Ultimate
Governor), who is both the wisdom and the power of God'.*
OSMOND

## WHAT IS INVOLVED IN GOVERNANCE?

**In the key text, Isaiah 9: 6-7,** *"For unto us a child is born, unto us a
son is given: and the government shall be upon his shoulder: and his name
shall be called Wonderful, Counselor, The Mighty God, The everlasting
Father, The Prince of Peace. Of the increase of his government and peace
there shall be no end, upon the throne of David, and upon his kingdom, to
order it, and to establish it with judgment and with justice from hencefortheven
forever. The zeal of the LORD of hosts will perform this".*

The fundamental or key purpose for the coming of the Lord Jesus
Christ is to provide *governance*. The qualities, which give Him the
capacity to achieve that, are then listed in the text.

The concept of government, according to Webster's New Students Dictionary, has certain vital elements, which are worth looking at.

It involves the exercise of authority and rulership. The mention of **throne and kingdom** in the text refers to this authority and rulership. Governance goes with the exercise of a mandate.

It involves policy formulation and implementation.

(**Judgment and Justice** in the text refers to careful analysis of issues and the making of prudent and right decisions to arrest situations. And secondly, to make sure decisions arrived at are properly carried out. These are leadership executions that are nothing but policy/law/rule formulation and implementation).

It involves utilization of resources for the good of people. (As a sequel from the preceding one, **to order** from the text refers to the organization of things towards a set goal. This implies the making sure that human and other resources are stringently organized to support the people, who mandated this authority over themselves).

There is also an element of time. (The element of time is indicated in the text by *from henceforth even forever more*. This time frame is essential for: the tracing of when the exercise of the said authority began; the measurement of how effective and efficient a particular reign has been able to operate; and also the measure of the extent to which a particular government has been able to achieve its goals within the period).

It involves decision making, directing, organizing and managing. (This is shown in the text by the phrase _to order it and establish it_. To put any enterprise in a particular order and to establish it involves all the skills and elements of management. Here all available resources and expertise are mobilized, enforced and brought to bear to make sure the desired goals are reached).

These elements cut across the individual level, family level, institutions, communities, nations and the world at large. An attempt to define governance may not be too easy. It may then be said to be the right to exercise control, authority, or dominion over the use of available resources towards a desired goal (policy) for the good of people over some time. In simple terms it is just **making sure** the resources we have are managed to our benefit.

As an individual, you possess the right to control your own life and manage what you have, although you will give account on the judgment day. In the same light, members of a family have the right to control and manage it. Institutions higher go by the same light. Experience and history should have taught us by now that, governance is not at its best at all in the world. From the world level coming down to the individual level, poor governance is witnessed all over the place. This is evidenced by the chaos and break down of the very fiber of progress in our society. You can think about wars, famine, racism, ethnic clashes, religious conflicts, disease, hunger, abject poverty, rape, incest, sexual perversions, robberies, corruption, witchcraft, thefts in the church, suicide, ritual murders, abortion, industrial and socio-political demonstrations, divorce tendencies, child and spousal abuse, drug addiction, ... The list could just go on and on.

The basic issue at stake here is that **mankind without God, is a huge fiasco - a chasing of the wind.** All the physical, biological, social sciences, technology and the engineering in our universities and polytechnics we boast of are inadequate. So do **all** the religious inclinations and involvement (Christian and non-Christian alike), which deny the Lordship of Jesus Christ.

## NATURE OF CHRIST

Jesus Christ possesses all authority. In Matt 28: 18, *Jesus said, ' All authority has been given to Me in heaven and on earth".* Also in Revelation 1: 17b, He echoes, *" Fear not; I am the first and the last".*

Thus Supreme authority does not belong to anybody, but the Lord Jesus Christ. The right to govern in itself emanates from Him to human beings. The exercise of power, authority, and dominion is in His sole custody.

From preceding pages, we acknowledge that God is wise, implying that He alone understands all things and knows how to skillfully, perfectly and appropriately apply that knowledge to life to accomplish the desired results. Therefore the right knowledge base, the skill, the right methodology, the right timing, the inner strength and urge any person would need to accomplish any task or any goal set in life comes from Him. This also means that the results will please Him, because it would be done His way and by His strength.

The Bible pictures Jesus Christ as the very Wisdom of God. In 1 Cor 1: 24, 30a, the Word of God declares that, *"But unto them which are called, both Jews and Greeks, Christ the power of God, and **the Wisdom of God**. But of Him are ye in <u>Christ Jesus, who of God is made unto us **Wisdom**...</u>"*

The scripture is clearly stating that Jesus Christ is the wisdom and the power of God. Whatever God wants to be done, the architect, the consultant, the executor and the very sustainer of the project is The Lord Jesus Christ. In John 1: 3, the Bible says that, *"All things were made by Him; and without Him was not anything made that was made"*. No wonder in harmony, the Holy Scripture said in Isaiah that the government shall be upon His shoulder.

Talking about policy formulation and implementation, I really wonder if any person could come up with any policy, which may even be close to that of Christ who is the very Wisdom of God. The policy could be personal, family, institutional, or community based. You need the directions of Christ. He also possesses and gives the strength by which we may do whatever we need to do according to His will. In Phil 4: 13, the Word says that, "*I can do all things through Christ who strengthens me*". John 15: 6b also reads that, *"For without Me ye can do nothing"*. This is The Lord Jesus Christ, the gift of God to you.

But I submit to you that you could do far more exceedingly than you are doing now if you will allow Christ to direct your life.

## THE ULTIMATE GOVERNOR

By now you may have caught the glimpse of what Jesus could do in terms of governance. He is the ultimate Governor. From Isaiah 9: 7a, the Bible declares that, "*Of the increase of his government and peace there shall be no end, upon the throne of David, and upon his kingdom, to order it, and to establish it with judgment and with justice from henceforth-even forever*".

We find what the scripture says He will do when He sits on the seat of David, when He comes to rule in the last days. We see continuous progression of proper governance and peace. We also discover that He will order and establish it. WOW! This is just beautiful. The Master manager at work: the proper ordering, directing, organizing, and establishment of the dominion of David when Jesus Christ is at the helm of affairs. The ultimate Governor is in action.

This is the picture when He occupies the throne of David. What about you and me? Are we people He doesn't want to assist or we haven't allowed him to? Do we cast our cares and worries upon Him (1 Pet 5:7)? In Matt 11: 28, Jesus invites, " *Come unto Me, all ye that labour and are heavy laden, and I will give you rest"*. There is no clearer invitation than this to all of us. <u>He only needs the seat of rule and control of your life.</u>

When you make Him the LORD or MASTER over your life, He will then have the right to begin to put things in shape for you, not only for today but also for eternity. He becomes the final authority in every decision you make. Your plans must be in pencil and you hand over the eraser to Him. All your attitudes, thoughts, actions, plans, etc., must be motivated by your desire to please Him. <u>Jesus governing you means you owe Him your deepest loyalty and allegiance.</u>

Don't forget that He has His working principles by which He goes about setting things in order. These principles of Christ are the best for mortal man. They are truths, which emanate from His infinite knowledge and wisdom as the Creator. Therefore there is no second choice to them. These are outlined in the Holy Scriptures. You need to discover them, internalize them, believe them and apply them to your life. Don't ever think that you're smarter than the Word of God, so sometime you consciously decide to do what is contrary to the scriptures. Jesus Christ is the Word of God. He therefore basically instructs people through the Holy Scriptures. So you accept these principles of righteousness, love them, be proud of them, and work with them. Remember that judgment and justice are the basis for His rule and kingdom. The Bible says, in Isaiah 9: 7b, "... *to order it, and to establish it **with judgment and with justice...**"*

Beloved its time we begin to acknowledge our need of the Savior. No amount of arguments pridefully advanced can change the tide. **You and I need God. We need Christ.** The scriptures rightly say that *'the government shall be upon His shoulder'*. In other words this gift of God is the One on whom proper governance rests. Without Him, with His principles and teaching thrown overboard by **apparent knowledge** and **modernity**, we are in serious trouble. The Creator has invested **all capacity of governance in Him**. You may try, but without Him it is bound to fail ultimately. Therefore the earlier you gave Him the chance the better. In Matt 9: 12-13a, *Jesus said, ' Those who are well have no need of a physician, but those who are sick. But go and learn what this means...'* Think about it!

As an individual, whatever you do, your ultimate success is in your being able to escape the judgment of the LORD. Besides all we want to achieve in this life, remember, *" we shall all stand before the judgment seat of Christ"* (Rom 14: 10). Thus ultimately, **the entire personal goal you could ever set for your life must tie in with issues of eternity.**

From here we are going to look at some titles of Jesus Christ which are essentially, descriptions of the nature of the work He does in any life which is yielded to Him to order, control, and establish.

# CHAPTER FOUR
# THE WONDERFUL

*'The unchanging Christ still proves His deity and saving power by working wonders and miracles in the lives of people'*

OSMOND

## WONDERS

The individual is surrounded by many events in life. Some of these events could be astonishing, surprising and amazing. Others could really take you off, thus very unusual and extra ordinary. They can cause you to ask many questions. Such events are termed as wonders. Sometimes we call them miracles. Things, which are usually beyond human capacity and comprehension at the time they occur, are what wonders is. Wonders! We are talking about miracles. Miracles do happen, and they happen to those who want them and satisfy the necessary conditions.

Some people go through life limiting themselves to just what they think the mortal person could do. We are made with some brains to think, to figure out things, to plan and manage our lives. Always remember God has not left us in the dark to live our lives without His directions and support. No matter what is happening in our lives, God is very much interested. The loving Father yearns that we could discover His working principles, directions, and awesome power made available to man (those who want it).

In Ephesians 1: 19, we read that, *"and what is the exceeding greatness of His power **to us-ward who believe**, according to the working of His mighty power."* We are talking about the availability of the power of God to meet the needs of the individual on earth. The key condition is: to those who believe. We are talking about the direct intervention of God in the life people. Have you imagined the extent to which God can go with you through Christ? Do you think the living God wants you to go through the pain and suffering alone? He is still working miracles through the person of Jesus Christ.

All the processes of life emanated from Him and are sustained by Him. Thus He determines how things must work. Think of the process of growth, decay, healing, restoration, and sustenance in the natural world. These processes are part of the awesome principles by which the universe works; they are under the control of the Creator to sustain His creation in the way He wants them to go. It is not beyond His capacity to step in to directly intervene in the affairs of life of individuals. If the intervention will give glory and honor to Him, and to bring relief and joy to His people, he will do it.

God is still the miracle working God. People try to deny this fact to their own peril. They ignorantly do this as a way of trying to kick off the challenge of Christianity and of Christ from their life entirely. The issue is, how far could you go as an individual to perfectly put things in order? To what extent could you go in spite of the negative tendencies (spiritual, physical, social, health, economic and cultural)? Let the Lord Jesus Christ into your situation.

## WHY IS JESUS CHRIST CALLED WONDERFUL?

Jesus Christ is the same yesterday, today and forever. He worked miracles in the past; He is still in that business today and will be about the same business on the morrow (Heb 13: 8). Skeptics ridicule miracles, by saying that we are in the scientific new age, so they are simply impossible. These people in addition, claim that not only is it not true but that they do not really matter today. Some of these people are in the church playing Christianity, but denying the very person who performs these miracles. Some of them, ironically, are even in the clergy. They say that it is only His teaching and examples on morality and productivity, which matter today. They claim miracles are okay for those who like magic, but eludes one from true religious insight; concluding that miracles are for those who are poor and weak-minded.

Jesus Christ was like any mere person when He was on earth in many ways, but He did many powerful miraculous deeds. These miracles undoubtedly proved His claim to deity. People who met with Him could not stop wondering who He really was and the source of His miraculous power. People today tend to completely disbelieve these miracles that they actually took place, but the people in His day did not have that chance because they happened. The skeptics doubt the wonders because they doubt HIM as being the LORD of the universe who has power over the very things He has made. The people in His day knew the miracles meant something beyond the ordinary.

The enemies of Jesus at that time could not deny His miracles. The acts He performed demanded supernatural explanation. To push Him away from acceptance, the critics concluded that He worked through the power of the devil (Matt 12: 24). **The fact still remains that *His enemies admitted* He was a miracle worker.**

The friends of Christ could not help it but wonder the kind of person He was to have the capacity for such miracles. Matthew 8 opens with a miracle of Christ demonstrating His power over natural elements:

*And, behold, there arose a great tempest in the sea, inasmuch that the ship was covered with the waves: but he was asleep. And His disciples came to Him, and awoke Him, saying, Lord, save: we perish. And He said unto them, why are ye fearful, O ye of little faith? Then he arose, and rebuked the winds and the sea; and there was great calm. But the men marveled, saying, **What manner of man is this**, that even the winds and the sea obey Him!*

That's the question His miracles forced out of people: what kind of person is He? Who is this miracle worker? Who is this wonder worker? Friends of Jesus concluded that He was of God, God in human flesh, but His enemies conclude He was of the devil. One option they did not have as well as we, is that Jesus Christ was just a fine guy who lived a good life and left behind some good teachings. This person had supernatural powers and claimed to be equal to God. Either we reject Him outright or we receive Him fully, worshipping Him as the LORD of the universe.

The miracles of Christ and His divine claims are the central teachings in the four gospels (Matthew, Mark, Luke and John), which we can never ignore today. Historical evidence from recently discovered manuscript fragments of the New Testament gospels confirms that these accounts of the life of Christ were written a few decades after they occurred. Thus these authors knew the events first hand, and what they wrote better fitted with the eyewitness account, as they were still alive, or they would straighten them up.

These miracles of Jesus Christ prove and confront us with the reality of God himself. Jesus shows by His miracles that He is the LORD of creation. In the miracles of Christ, we see invasion of nature by the One who is nature's designer, creator and rightful ruler.

In the Bible, there are two forms of miracles Jesus Christ performed and He is still performing them today. These miracles are: miracles of the old creation, and the miracle of the new creation.

## Old Creation Miracles

In these types of miracles, Jesus does the things that God does every time. He only does them instantly, directly and in small scale; what God does gradually, indirectly and on a worldwide scale. Whatever nature takes so long a time to accomplish, He Jesus possesses the power to get such things done in an instant. For example, when He changed water to wine, do not forget that God has being changing water into wine using vines and the natural processes rather than instant transformation.

Jesus used a few loaves of bread to feed 5000 people. God takes up little grains and seeds (planting materials) every year, and with the weather and the soil, He transform it gradually and naturally to feed over 6 billion people (Psalm 104: 14-15).

When Jesus calmed the storm with that short command, He did what God has been doing in that natural process every time by making sure every storm, which arises on the sea, is quieted. Jesus as creator possesses the power to get the process done in an instant, shrinking the time factor. Psalm 89: 8-9 says, *" O LORD God of hosts, who is a strong LORD like unto thee? or to thy faithfulness round about thee? Thou rulest the raging of the sea: when the waves thereof arise, thou stillest them"*. So in reality when they asked what manner of person He was, the answer is simply, LORD God of host; is the Lord Jesus Christ. He is God in human flesh.

Jesus always has very deep concern for the bodily needs of people. Concerning the miracles of healing of the body by Jesus; He does what He has been doing all through the centuries. He has put in our bodies the natural capacities to heal themselves. Think of the immune system and what it's capable of doing for the individual. You catch cold and you even do not know how you get well. You get a cut, bleed a little, you do not even know how the blood clots; why doesn't the bleeding continue? Jesus the healer is still in action, working in nature. He possesses the power to and chooses to heal instantly sometimes.

Miracles are not violations of natural laws. They are simply demonstrations of His Lordship over of nature. Whatever we call **laws of nature are just the patterns by which the *Creator has ordered His creation to operate.*** They are therefore not binding on Him in anyway. Jesus as God in human flesh only demonstrated His identity as the Lord of creation.

## NEW CREATION MIRACLES

The new creation is about restoration of things. The miracles of Christ also proved Him as the Maker and Master of creation. These miracles give a foretaste of the new creation, which the Word of God says will come in the future. These new creation miracles reverse the processes of disease, decay, and death, that so beset the created order after the fall of humanity (Rom 8: 18-23). All things will be made new (Rev 21: 4-5). Jesus brought back the dead to life.

Christ awakens the spiritually dead, in sins and trespasses, and morally bankrupt people through regeneration into the new life of holiness (Eph 2: 1-5, Rom 6: 4). The power of the resurrection of Christ works to make us **born again**. This is an empowerment to become sons and daughters of God unto nothing but a life of hope and good works to the praise of Him who thus recreated us (Eph 2:10). This is a foretaste of restoration to come. *"He is the resurrection and the life, he who believes in Him, though dead shall live again"* (John 11: 25). **This is the wonderful Jesus.**

## <u>What Wonders Could He Do In Your Life?</u>

I do not know what you are going through, but there is one thing that I know: Jesus has all power to change your situation around. He is the WONDERFUL. He echoes in Jeremiah 32: 27, " *Behold, I am the LORD, the God of all flesh: is there anything too hard for Me?"*

He has done it for many and He will do it for you. He loves you. There is nothing, absolutely, beyond His capability. You only have to do one thing: humbly submit to Him, trusting in Him and He shall perform. In Mark 9: 23, *"Jesus said unto him, if thou canst believe, **all*** *things are possible to him that believeth."* All things mean all things, including yours. The most seemingly impossible situations are even what He could do to prove Himself. He is the Lord.

Your situation is not hopeless as you may be thinking. It may be wayward children, dear parent, which is driving you crazy. It may be a bunch of quarrelsome and arrogant church leaders who do not understand your vision for the church, pastor. It may be the devil making all effort to tear your church apart, dear minister of the gospel. It could also be an irresponsible husband bewitched by a 'mini-skirted' secretary at his office, dear wife. It may a contentious, nagging spouse, beloved reader, who is causing your heartache. It could also be greedy, morally bankrupt subordinate officers bootlicking your position, dear manager. Whatever the case may be Jesus is still the Lord over all things (Rom 9: 5).

Beloved, the God of wonders, the Lord Jesus Christ is inviting you to a miraculous encounter in your life; if only…He says in Matt 11: 28, *"Come unto Me, all ye that labour and are heavy laden and I will give you rest".* Shall we pause for some prayer? Commit your entire being to the Lord, every aspect of your life, right now.

# CHAPTER FIVE
# THE COUNSELLOR

*'We have racism, wars, famine, disease, higher divorce rate, street kids, child labor, suicides, rape, all because we have* **counsel bankruptcy'**

OSMOND

*'Jesus understands all things, knows all things; therefore perfect counsel to skillfully apply knowledge to deal with issues of life can then logically emanate from Him, and nobody else.'*

OSMOND.

## WHAT IS COUNSEL?

An attempt to look at the meaning of counsel from dictionaries and concordances produced some interesting ideas like:

- Advice given, especially as a result of consultation

- Purpose of God

- Most secret resolutions

- Policy or plan of action or behavior

- Lawyer engaged in the management of a case in court

Of all these attempted definitions of counsel, one basic idea deduced in summary is clear: that is to say that **counsel is the advice given or taken to facilitate a plan of action in the management of an issue.**

Thus first and foremost, counsel is a piece of information. That information, if accepted has the capacity to bring increase to you or to damage you. All the pieces of information, ideas, and principles which people use in the governing of their actions could all be classified as counsel. We have to bear in mind these ideas are accepted by the individual as a basis for actions.

As already said, the counsel could do you good or otherwise. The type of benefits a counsel could bring depends on its source. For it to bring you good and lasting benefits, the source must be good and dependable. The counsel in itself does not do anything but for the resolve or the choice made based on it. Life is made up of choices; the quality of the choices determines the quality of our lives. The quality of the choices depends also on the quality of counsel we receive. If the counsel is reliable, we get established in whatever we are doing. The Bible says in Proverbs 15: 22, *"Without counsel purposes are disappointed: but in the multitude of counselors they are established."* Thus the success or otherwise of any plans we may have depends on the counsel we receive. Through them we get ourselves established. As the counsels therefore are many, we obtain varied choices from which we make our resolve.

There are many things we need counsel about. The Bible says in Hosea 4: 6a, " *My people are destroyed for lack of knowledge...*" Because of knowledge deficiency, many endeavors of people are thrown overboard entirely or they end in shambles. It could be marriage, parenting, social life, job management, financial management etc. The world is in turmoil today because of inadequate counsel: in terms of quantity and quality. We have racism, wars, famine, disease, higher divorce rate, street kids, child labor, suicides, rape, all because we have **counsel bankruptcy**. This is a hard fact society should accept and determine a way out.

## Who Is a Counselor?

A counselor could be said to be <u>someone who can give an expert advice about something</u>. Thus the person must possess enough knowledge and experience in that field, to enable him/her to render a quality counsel in that particular field of life. There are professional counselors though, but what are we seeing in our society today? What is really gone amiss? I strongly submit that either they are not potentially resourced enough or people are not simply making use of them or both.

The counselor must possess in-depth knowledge, experience, skill to communicate, and expertise in dealing with issues that pertain to every area of human life. You would have realized that this is not that easy as in this universe we have the physical and the spiritual dimensions to life. There are two worlds as the Holy Scriptures makes it so plain and clear. In Colossians 1: 16, the Bible says that,

*" For by Jesus Christ were all things created, that are in heaven, and that are in earth, **visible and invisible**, whether they be thrones, or dominions, or principalities, or powers: all things were created by Him and for Him."*

We see here that besides human beings there are other beings in the universe as well. Not only are they in the system but that whether we like it or not they have some considerable influence on humans. There are only two spiritual kingdoms in existence. The kingdom of light whose king is Jesus Christ and the kingdom of darkness whose king is the devil. The Bible says thus about Christians, " *God hath delivered us from the power of darkness, and hath translated us into the kingdom of His dear son: in whom we have redemption through his blood, even the forgiveness of sins"(*Col 1: 13-14).

The invisible world of darkness is directly opposing humanity, with their human agents though, to frustrate the plans of Jehovah for mankind. That is why the Bible says in Ephesians 6: 12, *"For **we** wrestle not against flesh and blood, but against principalities, against powers, against the rulers of the darkness of this world, against spiritual wickedness in high places."* These dark forces oppose every human being on earth. You can assume they don't even exist; even decide to ignore them, but

43

the fact of the matter is that they work to prevent you from attaining or realizing your God appointed **earthly** and **eternal** destinies.

So life, my dear reader, is not just job, money, cars, sex, pomp and pageantry or just goal-setting-achievement matters only, as some might think. The principles of life, the counsel that drive people to choose to get these things by whichever means (whether fair or foul, even to kill) they see fit is not a good counsel. These propensities fuel the sex abuse, 'shaded' pornography in the name of fashion, greed, corruption, lust, murder, and war and so on, we witness today in our world, but this world is created to be enjoyed by God. These counsels are then from the camp of the devil, the Bible calls **worldly**. So you have realized that even the source of the counsel even matters a lot. Therefore getting most adequately resourced, as a counselor, is not just an exposure to a little aspect of life; be it medicine, law, teaching, psychology, or whatever. Even the medics, if sincere to themselves would agree with me that its not just tablets/capsules/injections which cause healing in the body but also the psychology (soul influence) of the person.

## THE ULTIMATE COUNSELOR

So far, one can see that, you and I need a counselor who can give adequate and dependable counsel to govern our lives. We need a counselor who possess the requisite knowledge base, skill, experience, wisdom, tact, foresight, love, and deeper insight into every area of human life; visible and invisible. We need such a person whose counsel can really take us far. The counsel from that person should make us take very wise choices in life from all perspectives. We are talking about real safety and responsible decisions, physically, socially, financially, healthwise, spiritually, and managerially or whichever area of endeavor you can think of. The counsel must suffice not only for today's basic sustenance and luxury, but should also be adequate for the judgment to come as well. If your counsel has no eternal perspective, then forget it. Safe counsel must take into account the judgment to come. **So if you get all your goals met and you end up eternally in the lake of fire; the Bible emphatically declares that you are not wise (Matt 16:26).** We're discussing the Ultimate Counselor.

The descriptions given above can fit nobody, but the only King of kings, the Lord of lords, and the only Potentate of time (1 Tim 6:15), the Lord Jesus Christ. The holy scriptures declare the Lord Jesus Christ as the Counselor; and truly He is. In fact, He possesses all the qualities necessary for it, and the infallible Word has thus declared Him to be so. The Gift of God, the Lord Jesus Christ is:

- The truth (John 14: 6)

- The Way (John 14: 6)

- The Life (John 14: 6)

- The Alpha and the Omega (Rev 22: 12-13)

- The Creator and Sustainer of the universe (Col 1: 16-17)

- All wise God (Dan 2: 20-21)

- All knowing God (Isaiah 46: 10)

Jesus Christ is the living embodiment of truth; all that He is made of, whatever He stands for and advocates are the ultimate reality. His counsel is what is called the reality. You might not just understand His counsel or appreciate them now; but in the final analysis you will realize that He is, and His counsel is the TRUTH. His name is the Word of God (Rev 19: 11-16). This simply implies that **if a person is going contrary to His principles, then the person is simply under deception and does not have the truth.**

Jesus, as the Way, defines for mankind the divinely prescribed code of life. The Bible clearly states this, in John 1: 4,9, *"In Him is life; and the life was the light of men. That was **the true Light, which lighted every man that cometh into the world.**"* He shows us the way to the Father. This is Jesus the Gift of God. The hard implicational fact is that those who reject the counsel of Christ are simply LOST.

Life is Jesus Christ. In Him is life (John 1: 4). As the embodiment of life He sustains all things. His counsel therefore brings life, vitality, and sustenance to every area of the life of men. He thus gives eternal life to as many as take His counsel. Those who reject Him do so to their own peril; bringing death, decay, corruption, failure and eternal damnation to their life.

Alpha and Omega, the beginning and the end, that is Jesus Christ (Rev 22: 12-13, 16). Christ determines all that the entire time and eternity means. If ever anything could happen, it will never take Him by surprise. That simply means that every activity of all persons, visible and invisible, will ultimately conform to what Jesus Christ determines. So the consequence of putting His counsel off is obvious. The entire universe is His. The past, the present and the future are all in His custody. The First and the Last; everything emanates from Him and will culminate in Him.

Jesus is the creator and sustainer of all things (Col 1:16-17). Someone created His world to put you in and you think you have experienced His earth and known so much to even ignore Him. This is ridiculous. In fact, all that we could **ever** discover in this universe, is that Jesus Christ is that ultimate truth and counselor humans have being groping in the ages to discover in science, religion, occult, new-aging, neo-sciences, metaphysics, traditionalism, Hinduism, Buddhism, lodges, etc. Beloved, pause and reflect on this issue seriously.

The all-wise God we talk about is the same Lord Jesus Christ (1 Tim 6: 14-16; Rom 16: 25-27). That is the reason why the Father even does not do anything without the counsel of Jesus Christ (John 1: 4), the architect of the universe. Jesus Christ is the very Wisdom and the Word of God. The Bible makes it clear that Jesus is the very wisdom

47

of God (1 Cor 1: 24). Jesus understands all things, knows all things; therefore perfect, skilful application of knowledge to deal with issues can then logically emanate from Him, and nobody else.

Just look at this person called Jesus Christ. If we are then talking of the ultimate counselor, it is nobody but the Lord Jesus Christ. This Gift of God is just for you. Truly you and I need His counsel every moment of our life.

# CHAPTER SIX
# THE MIGHTY GOD

*'Jesus Christ, the mighty one in battle is always seeking to show Himself strong on your behalf'*

2 CHRONICLES 16:9

## WHO IS A MIGHTY PERSON?

We speak of **mighty** when we are referring to:

- Having power to do something

- Great or imposing in size or strength or extent

- Very or extremely (as an adjective)

- Having vigor

- Prevailing in battle or war

It carries with it a sense of achievement of **feat**. If we are then saying that someone is mighty, then in summary, *the person possesses the ability or capacity to prevail over circumstances or challenges.* 'Might' could be looked at from different perspectives; but all fall under the same concept. We can talk about wealth, knowledge, strength, authority, skill, wisdom, power and size. In other words the mighty person possesses a positional and a confrontational advantage over the opponent or adversary or anything standing in the way of the person. The adversary could be anything; from demons to diseases, from falsehood to weather, from poverty to failure, from sin to any challenge one could be facing.

The situation in question will determine the kind of positional advantage we are talking about. For instance, in an organization, the director will be seen to be mightier than the clerk. This is because the director could decide the working conditions of the organization, which can either positively or negatively affect the clerk, even to lay him or her off. Here we say that the director is mightier than the clerk. Thus the positional advantage is **authority.** We could also look at the devil and God. God has the positional advantage over the devil in terms of authority, because God as the Creator uncreated and sustainer of all life forms, including that of the devil, is then in authority.

When two opponents who are about equal standing are contesting in a fight, the one with the greatest **skill, and strength** (stamina and health), wins the fight. In this situation, the advantage is skill and stamina. We could have two artisans or manufacturers competing for customers for their products, the one who shows more skill in the product and service will definitely pull more customers. Skill is the cutting edge of productivity. The Bible thus declares, in Eccl 10: 10, *"If* *the iron be blunt, and he do not whet the edge, then must he put to more strength: but wisdom is profitable to direct."* Therefore skill or stamina could be seen as a form of might.

If we are to take a look at students, taking an examination, the one who excels in that particular test is then considered as the stronger or the mightier. Here the positional advantage is the **knowledge** base. Thus knowledge is considered then as might. Two people may encounter the same problem; one may commit suicide because of not knowing what to do, hence feeling hopeless or helpless. The other fellow may solve the said problem and just go on with life; thus prevailing over the problem. Thus knowledge is power or might. By knowledge, as much as we know, we have mastered the earth. By what we know, we are able to come by enough income to cater for our families (nuclear and external) and ourselves. Knowledge then gives us competitive positional advantage. **If someone is doing something better than you, then the person simply may know something you do not know.** Then in that particular endeavor, we will say that the person is mightier than you are.

**Wisdom** is also seen as might. The ability to solve problems, which we call wisdom, is a vital ingredient in successful, vibrant and peaceful life, which every well-meaning person desires to have. It is in two-fold. The first is the ability to handle situations, which may arise accidentally. The second is ability to perceive possible problems or situations, having a sense of vision or foresight, and planning ahead to avoid them. Possessing this quality is of course a comparative positional advantage over opponents or adversaries who might be foolish or worse still stupid. Wisdom is then the principal thing, and of course, a form of might. In other words the people who are wise are able to surmount adverse circumstances better than their fellows with less wisdom.

**Wealth** is another form of might. Wealth is basically defined as abundance of possessions or resources. An individual, possessing resources to meet any need or challenge in life is considered mighty. The resource could be tangible, abstract or virtual. The resource can be spiritual power, health, money, position of authority, minerals, knowledge, food, water, IT, machinery, wisdom, creative intelligence, etc. If someone could command for things to be available to meet a need, then that person is mighty. Thus possessing the capability to make things happen when necessary or get things done at the right time constitutes might. The ability to call things into being, because one has the resources in abundance and also the authority to command is a mark of might. **Thus wealthy people are mighty persons.**

Might possesses the capacity to win or prevail in a battle against one's adversaries. Life is war. Wars are made up of many battles. The battles are the various challenges we face at one point in life or the other. The mighty person is the one who has the ability to prevail in all circumstances. We could be talking about spiritual or physical dimensions in life, but the mighty will always prevail. The challenge could be a sinful habit, poverty, disease, wayward spouse, divorce tendencies, rebellious children, poor output of work, witchcraft, enchantments, arm of oppression, threats, church breaking up, financial bankruptcy, etc. Whatever the case may be the mighty shall prevail.

There is something worth noting about might. The Bible echoes in Romans 15: 1 that, *"We then that are strong **ought** to bear the infirmities of the weak, and not to please ourselves."* The Word of God sets forth a principle, which binds on the supposedly strong or mighty well meaning persons. It is a moral obligation, rational deduction, natural expectation and a logical sequence for persons who are in the position of might to support the weak. Extension of a hand of support for other people in trouble demonstrates how strong, in reality we are. We are just selfish, self-centered and with narrow perception about life if we cannot help others. **We could then conclude that, the more mighty you are the more others will benefit from you.** Therefore mighty people stand to save and salvage the situation of the weak. Such a person **must be able to protect and defend the weak**. Such efforts from the strong are then directed to strengthen the weak in their spheres of weakness. Remember that we are talking about every sphere of human life: physical, spiritual, emotional, social, managerial, etc. **Therefore a <u>savior</u> must be a mighty person.**

We thus see what a mighty person is. If anyone wants to acclaim strength or might, the person must begin to look at all the areas of the concept of might. The person must make a self-check to see whether he or she is really a mighty person. If you do not fully qualify, then you have to humble yourself to a mightier person to lift you up. Dear reader, I will be introducing to you such a **Mightier Person** very soon. In fact, He is the gift we have being talking about all this while. The Lord Jesus Christ is that Mighty One.

## IS JESUS CHRIST THE MIGHTY GOD?

The answer to this question, I think is simply to just check whether Christ Jesus possesses the qualities of God and a mighty person. The Bible gives us a vivid picture about who Christ really is in this regard.

In Colossians 1:16, the Bible says that,

"*For by Him were all things created, that are in heaven and that are in earth, visible and invisible, whether they be thrones, or dominions, or principalities, or powers: all things were created by Him, and for Him.*"

This text is simply saying that Jesus Christ is first the Creator, and secondly, all things belong to Him. Period! Psalm 24:1 says, "*The earth is the LORD's and the fullness thereof; the world, and they that dwell therein.*" Also in Psalm 50:12. Here the Bible is simply echoing that the Lord Jesus Christ is God and He is just **wealthy**. He possesses all things, so we could conclude that He is the Almighty.

The Word of God says in Matt 28: 18, *"And Jesus spoke unto them, saying, **All authority is given unto Me** in heaven and in earth."* We also read in Phil 2:10-11, *"That **at the name of Jesus every knee should bow**, of things in heaven, and things in earth, and things under the earth; And that **every tongue should confess that Jesus Christ is Lord**, to the glory of God the Father".*

From the two scriptures, the Bible makes it unequivocally clear that Jesus Christ is the sole custodian of all that we refer to as authority, the **Absolute Master**. Jesus Christ is the King of all the kings and Lord of all the lords. He is then all-powerful and almighty. He must then necessarily be obeyed.

By the fact that He is the creator and sustainer of the universe, all things must then submit to Him. He is truly mighty (Rev 1: 8). Can the creature then rebel against the Creator and go scot-free? NO! As Isaiah 45:9 says, *"Woe to him that striveth with his Maker! Let the potsherd strive with the potsherds of the earth. **Shall the clay say to Him that fashioned it, What makest thou?** Or thy work, he has no hands?"* This must not be; such clay will definitely not prosper.

God possesses all wisdom. Jesus is the very wisdom of God. Thus He is the very personal embodiment of the faculty of the Godhead called wisdom. Therefore the very capacity of God having to do with understanding all things, skillfully and perfectly appropriating all knowledge to accomplish the determinate divine purposes of the

Godhead is the Lord Jesus Christ. If wisdom then is a form of might, we shall obviously then conclude that Jesus is the almighty. Jesus Christ is the omniscient God.

In terms of war, God is the almighty. The Bible says in Psalm 24:7-10, *"Lift up your heads O you gates and be lifted up you everlasting doors! And the King of glory shall come in. Who is this King of glory? The LORD strong and mighty, the LORD mighty in battle. Who is this King of glory? The LORD of hosts, He is the King of glory."*

We read in Joshua 5:13,14, that when Joshua was scouting the outskirts of Jericho, this Captain of the hosts, who met Joshua and accepted worship from him is no other person but Jehovah, the pre-incarnated Jesus Christ (Christophany). The name Lord of hosts or Jehovah Lord Sabaoth refers to God as the fighter or the Man of war, who leads His people to battle in victory. There is a beautiful picture of Him from Revelation 19: 11-16,

*"Now I saw heaven opened and behold, a white horse. And He who sat on him was **called Faithful and True, and in righteousness He** judges and **makes war**. His eyes were like a flame of fire, and on His head were many crowns. He had a name written that no one knew except Himself. **He was clothed with a robe dipped in blood**, and His name is called the **Word of God. And the armies in heaven**, clothed in fine linen, white and clean, **followed Him** on white horses. Now out of His mouth goes a sharp sword, that with it he should strike the nations. And He*

*Himself will rule them with a rod of iron. He Himself treads the winepress of the fierceness and wrath of almighty God.* **And He has on His robe and on His thigh a name written: KING OF KINGS AND LORD OF LORDS."**

What we read here is a confirmation that the Lord Jesus Christ is THE LORD MIGHTY IN BATTLE. He cannot lose in any battle; therefore those who are of heavenly citizenship (Phil 3:20) and the heavenly army also know no defeat. In His Name Jesus every knee, in whichever realm of existence, shall bow. **<u>Absolutely</u> nothing can stop Him.** Jesus Christ is the mighty God we talk about always ( Rom 9:5).

In reality, the Lord Jesus is the most powerfully resourced military commander and He possesses the most equipped and skillful army in the whole universe.

In Rev 17: 14, we read," *These shall make war with the Lamb, and the* **Lamb shall overcome them: for He is Lord of lords, and King of kings:** *and <u>they that are with Him are called, and chosen, and faithful</u>.* His arsenals and the weaponry at His disposal as the Creator of the universe is just awesome and unparalleled; in whatever terms you may want to imply. We read from 2 Cor 10:4 that, *"The* **weapons** *of our warfare are not carnal but they* **are <u>mighty through God</u> to the pulling down of strong holds."** In fact the warfare He is engaged in now and ever could be engaged in is already concluded. In Rev 12: 11, the Bible emphatically makes it clear that, those who even follow Him overcame the enemy, the devil, by the blood of Christ Jesus. **Jesus Christ the Lord is mighty.**

From the discussion above, it is clear that, with all the concepts involved, we have just one conclusion to make and that is Jesus is the mighty God. He possesses all knowledge, wisdom, resources, power, skill, authority, stature, and any other quality you could ever think of or imagine that gives one the capacity to be the mighty God and of course the mighty Savior. You and I need Him.

## Jesus Christ The Mighty God On Your Side

Jesus is the mighty God, that is true and of course a powerful good news for all humanity. Imagine if the devil were to have this title and qualities; you and I would have been in the deepest recesses of trouble. But thanks be to God who has not allowed it to be so, rather that this same Jesus is the Savior, Salvager and Lord. Thus bringing to bear all His attributes and characteristics on our circumstances for our good and benefit.

This can only be when any person decides to be on His side wholly. Some people are on the side of Christ only when they are in the church room, or when things appear to be in their favor. Dear reader, you may not be of the Christian inclination, but the issue is still clear, that Jesus Christ is for all humanity. He is not just for only Jews, Caucasians or for that matter any particular group of people. You may also have being confessing Christ, but remember Jesus demands total allegiance and dependence on Him.

The bible says in 2 Chro 16: 9 that, *"For the eyes of the **LORD** run to and fro throughout the whole earth, **to shew Himself strong in the behalf of them whose heart is perfect toward Him**. Herein thou hast done foolishly: therefore from henceforth thou shalt have wars."*

This same Lord is ever ready to just prove Himself mighty, dear reader, to exhibit all His might and power on your behalf. WOW! Think about this!

The keys to having the mighty Jesus fighting for you are found in the text above: *them whose heart is perfect towards Him.* Here is it, perfect heart, a heart full of trust and faith in Jesus. A heart that is bent on just pleasing Jesus (2 Tim 2:4, John 8:29). A heart that totally acknowledges what He is and what He could do (Heb 11: 6). A heart that totally depends on Him and Him alone (John 15: 5) is the secret. A heart that sincerely seeks to conform to Christ in attitude, conduct, conversation and thoughts is what makes the difference. He is looking for the heart that yearns to allow Him to just manifest Himself through that life. The key is the heart full of holiness and dependence on God. The mighty God is seeking for people with servant hearts.

It is there and then that we shall have, *"Thus saith the LORD unto you, Be not afraid or dismayed by reason of this great multitude; for the battle is not yours, but belongs God's* (2 Chro 20: 15)"

Prepare the Lord Jesus a place to stay in your heart. Make Him, the gift of God, your inheritance. He will then be on your side so that you can reign and prevail in this life. Psalm 16:5-9 gives us a summary of our discussion so beautifully, *"The Lord is the portion of mine inheritance and of my cup: thou maintainest my lot. The lines are fallen unto me in pleasant places; yea, I have a goodly heritage. I will bless the LORD, who hath given me counsel: my reins also instruct me in the night seasons. I have set the LORD always before me: because He is at my right hand, I shall not be moved. Therefore my heart is glad, and my glory rejoiceth: my flesh also shall rest in hope."*

Beloved here you are. Receive this gift Jehovah has for you and you will never regret you did; for your life will not be the same, but change for the better.

When Jesus Christ is made the true Lord in your life, He makes you mighty and unbeatable as well (Rom 8:37). You become a champion and you shall reign in this life and hereafter. Remember He leads His followers on white horses to victory.

# CHAPTER SEVEN
# THE EVERLASTING FATHER

*'Christ as your everlasting Father simply means to have that covenant relationship with Him, which gives Him the spiritual legal right and responsibility to exercise over your life all fatherhood demands'*

OSMOND

*'The love of Christ causes Him to deeply yearn to care for you and to lavish all He has on you'*

OSMOND.

## WHO IS A FATHER?

The word father is a title given to male persons who are attached to us in a special relationship. The Webster's New Students Dictionary defines a father as: "

- A male parent

- One who cares for another as a male parent

- The originator, author, founder or producer

- God"

The concepts derived from the dictionary definition of the word father, firstly talk about someone of the male gender who gives seed to a female for reproduction. Here the relationship is biological. Thus we find in this aspect of the concept, fathers been all males who have impregnated females to have children with them. We say any male whose gametes together with that of a female have produced a human child is then a father. This bracket includes the sane and the insane, the rich and the poor, the whole and the invalid, the young and the old, the responsible and the irresponsible, etc. In this biological sense there can be only one father and no more. So whether by genetic engineering process or whatever means by which the baby comes to the world, the fact still remains that the father is one and only one. This fatherhood mentioned, is not, by sequence limited to just birth, but also how this offspring is cared for to maturity. **The _right_ of giving birth to a child also automatically ushers this parent into the _responsibility_ of caring for that child.**

A father is seen in this double sense; a biological relationship followed by care. We have a picture of not just giving birth to but also exercising proper oversight of a child for a sound growth and development to maturity. This includes protection, provision, education, health, etc. Thus the child must be able to capture this picture of a supposed father in his/her memories for good; someone called **daddy,** who connotes a shield, inspiration, support, input, etc., yes, yes DAD.

So if you are a father, then know what you are really into as a result of your right to have a child.

In another sense we could have a father by a special non-biological relationship. This happens when a male, who is older or in a higher position than us, assumes a caring attitude towards us in such a way as to befit a natural father. We naturally, have a feeling that the person is a father to us. We sometimes even call them daddy unconsciously. This is because this sense is derived from the fulfillment we socially, economically, educationally and spiritually receive from such persons. It is then only natural to feel and call these persons fathers.

This is irrespective of whether or not our biological fathers are present or agree. It's a natural consequence. These sorts of fathers are seen as mentors and personal counselors. They are people we go to, most of the time, when we are in our deepest anxieties. We respect them and treat them so well, even sometimes better than our true biological parents (which is biblically bad anyway, as we are enjoined to honor our parents unconditionally, Exodus 20:12, Ephesians 6: 2)

Remember the sense of value we place on this class of fathers is based on the self-imposed responsibility of care they exercise over us. We usually do not ask for the responsibility of care, but often these people voluntarily, out of love, take the choice of responsibility over us. Most of these people are pastors, whether by vocation or by call or both. So by responsibility of care, we call such men fathers. By the fatherly care they exercise over us, we also reciprocate with the kind of attitude, which are befitting to real biological parents.

The word father also carries with it the concept of someone who borne, initiated, created or the 'first-hand-bringer-forth' of a concept or an idea from the virtual into tangible reality. This is the area of originality and authorship of thought. Thus anyone who is seen as the author of, the founder of or the producer of something is said to be the father of that particular thing. We could then say that Albert Einstein is the father of the Theory of Relativity.

This realm of fatherhood stems from the idea that, children are born from the seed of the man. The person we call Jesus Christ is the only one born with the seed of the woman (Gen 3: 15). Thus the initiator and the seed supplier for a child to be born is then the man. It is only the woman who also possesses within her the capacity to nurture this offspring to birth and well beyond. Therefore anyone who becomes the originator of a concept, which is brought forth to reality, is said to be a/the father of that thing. Anyone whose contribution is in no small way significantly affecting an institution, a body of thought, a process or even a city or a nation is also thought of as a father of that thing.

God is seen as father over all things. This thought is not at all false but it's a living reality in its broadest sense. The Creator of all things, whether real or virtual, is the Lord God Almighty, as biblically proven earlier. So God is seen as the Father of all things.

## THE RESPONSIBILITIES OF A FATHER

The responsibilities of a father are numerous. Notwithstanding all could be summed up into five main categories, namely: headship over child, security provider, provider of money and material things, role model and lastly a trainer of the child.

The father is the one entrusted with the headship of the whole family, according to scripture. In Ephesians 5:22-24, we read thus, *'Wives, submit yourselves unto your husbands, as unto the Lord. For the husband is the head of the wife, even as Christ is the head of the church: and He is the Savior of the body. Therefore as the church is subject unto Christ, so let the wives be to their own husbands in everything.'*

This is Bible. Here the headship of the husband or the father of the home is not by income nor race nor education nor stature nor... but by right of marriage, God has ordained the man to be. Note that abuse of that position or irresponsible handling of it does not nullify its ordination, as long as the marital relationship is there. Improper acceptance and handling of this divine order in the home create problems.

As the father, then, it becomes your responsibility to provide **leadership** to the child. This leadership involves the designing and realizing of a vision and goal for life for the child. This goal must be acceptable, responsible and sustaining. This enterprise then aims at making the child into an adult the society can be proud of; and also approved of by God. So it is not just a question of boasting of having 'schoolful' of kids, but it's an awesome responsibility of making sure they are **properly** brought up._

Fatherhood also involves the provision of security for the child. From the Webster's dictionary, security carries the ideas of, 'state of being secure; freedom from anxiety; safety; surety; protection; and then measures of protection.' This involves immediate and future considerations. The father must necessarily do everything, which needs to be done to ensure the safety of the child now and the morrow. The dangers involved here could be physical harm (injuries), poor anatomic and mental health, and diseases, destitution, poverty, spiritual bondage and associated problems, academic and intellectual incapacitation, etc.

We could be talking about the father providing food, clothing and shelter, which are basic. We should not forget other essentials such as wholesome education (adequate information), enabling environment and exposure, proper peer and multimedia censorship, confidence-building measures, decision-making and problem-solving techniques, etc. Thus nothing must be left unchecked to see to it that your ward is safe for now and the future.

Fatherhood over a child involves financial commitment. The bible says in Ecclesiastics 10:19, *'A feast is made for laughter, and wine maketh merry: but money answereth all things.'* Thus in life money is used in all things we do. You can talk about anything, from education to religion, from archeology to zoology, in fact everything humans do involve money. You can think about this yourself; if you discover anything we do which does not involve money directly or indirectly, I will be just glad to hear from you about it. Here we are talking about the father being adequately resourced financially to support this child in everything involving money. Pay all bills; provide all necessary things and services for the child.

The fatherhood enterprise also involves role modeling. The father must be a shining example to this child in all things commendable. The father must provide a source of hope, encouragement and inspiration for this child. The father is to be someone whose personal achievements, attitudes to work and life generally, become a great challenge to the child to equal or do better.

Better still, the Dad is to be the kind of person who must be in the position to mentor this offspring. The child must see the dad as someone he/she trusts to the point that she/he could confide in you; share personal fears, anxieties, hopes and aspirations with for guidance and direction. The bible says in Ephesians 6:4, *'And, ye fathers, <u>provoke not your children to **wrath**</u>: but bring them up in the nurture and admonition of the Lord.'* The father is not someone who rather provokes the child to anger, despair, despondency, self-pity, poor self-concept and destruction.

Another grueling task for fathers is the job of training or disciplining of children. According to Webster's dictionary, discipline carry with it the idea of: 'teaching, learning, training that molds or perfects, punish, orderly conduct gained by training and system of rules governing conduct.' Here we see fathers are to consciously and purposely seek to put into order the behavior and conduct of their wards towards a specific desired form or mold of conduct. Not just leaving the kid at the mercy of a house-help or nannies, nor is it an issue of child abuse. Rather it should be out of love, training, teaching, rebuking, and by all socially acceptable and biblically approved methods making sure the child behaves and grows into an acceptable mold of character. Out of ignorance, unguided and misinformed passions some call love, career and business or even worse still 'I sure must make it syndrome', many ignore the discipline of their children. Some parents leave their wards spoilt and pampered and at the mercy of the TV, the Internet and the kids' peer groups. Proper, moral upbringing of children is now sacrificed for the sake of money and personal ambitions and passions. Nobody is in the house to make sure the kids are really doing the right thing, oh God have mercy.

Fathers discipline your children. Provision of food, clothes, shelter and school fees or supplies is not enough. A lot of societal chaos and heartaches are just the consequences of parents who do not discipline their wards. **It always takes a disciplined parent to see the essence of discipline, in order to discipline their wards.**

Disciplining is a primary responsibility. Remember any bad behavior from a child is from ignorance, curiosity, need or rebellion. Find the source and deal with it accordingly. If it is ignorance, provide adequate knowledge through a conscious sustainable effort of teaching. If it is curiosity, provide guidance and factual information, relating it to truth and natural consequences of their actions. If it is from a need, provide the necessary need to solve the problem. Rebellion demands a rebuke, teaching and encouragement to righteousness.

Being a father is really a huge business. Assuming you were to have a father who was able to fulfill these demands perfectly to the letter, how do you think you would have being and felt? Although you may be an adult, there is still a Father who wants and actually yearns to provide you with all this support we need as mortal persons in order to make the most of life from the eternal perspective. Beloved, God cares. In fact He really cares for you as an individual.

## HAVING CHRIST JESUS AS YOUR EVERLASTING FATHER

To have Christ as your everlasting Father simply means to have that covenant relationship with Him, which gives Him the spiritual legal right and responsibility to exercise over your life all the fatherhood demands discussed. The relationship is primarily spiritual. This is so as

God is a spirit, and as a human being is essentially a spirit, God relates to our spirit-man. We read in John 4:24, *'God is a Spirit: and they that worship Him must worship Him in spirit and in truth.'*

Oh! How one may wish Christ would be a Father to him/her. Look at what He is and what He could do for you. It is not late at all if you want to establish this relationship. This actually starts from the salvation of your soul. The Bible says that as many as believe in Him, even those that believe in His Name, He gave them the right to become the children of God (John 1:12). It is therefore necessary to surrender your total being to Jesus Christ as your personal Lord and Savior. Some people think they do not need any savior to save them. Beloved reader, if you cannot see yourself as a sinner who needs to be saved from sin and it's effects, Christ cannot save you (Matt 18:10-14). Note that **Christ is the only one who can save** (Acts 4:10-12), and trust the salvation of your soul in His hands (Rom 10:9-11, Heb 7:25). You cannot save yourself. Hence you cannot be a child of God without Christ.

Remember that all people are creatures made in the image of God but not all are the sons and daughters of God. It takes faith in Christ, the only begotten Son of God, to establish the relationship, which makes God your Father and you a child and co-heir with Christ (Gal 3:26-29; 4:4-7).

It is only when you become a child of God that His fatherhood responsibilities over you also start. You need to give your life to Christ.

He loves you so much. He died for you so that you could have this relationship established, if you wish, in order to appropriate into a tangible sense, His eternal love and lavishness in your personal life.

To establish and **maintain** this relationship with Christ as your everlasting Father demands a total commitment and allegiance to God, and a separation from whatever the Bible calls the world system. The Bible says in 2 Corinthians 6:14-18, *'Be ye not unequally yoked together with unbelievers: for what fellowship hath righteousness with unrighteousness?' And what communion hath light with darkness? And what concord hath Christ with Belial? Or what part hath he that believed with an infidel? And what agreement hath the temple of God with idols? For you are the temple of the living God; as God hath said, I will dwell in them, and walk in them; and I will be their God, and they shall be my people. 'Wherefore come out from among them, and be ye separate, saith the Lord, and touch not the unclean thing; and I will receive you, and will be a Father unto you, and ye shall be my sons and daughters, saith the Lord Almighty.'*

Any sincere reader could deduce that just confessing Christ and playing church, trying to fulfill personal ambition is not the matter. God is saying that, to be His child, you must separate yourself from sinful life and worldliness; and then He will receive you. IT IS NON NEGOTIABLE, NO COMPROMISE! It does not matter how many years you have been in the church, you could even be in the clergy, you may be accepted by the society, etc. The standards of God are non-negotiable; it does not know modernity. So if what you are doing today is not what Christ recommends, then…The hallmark of the children of God is holiness (2 Tim 2:19). Do you desire to be a child of Christ for Him to 'parent' you? Then seriously consider what the Word of God is saying: (**John 15:18,19, James 4:4, 1 John 2:15; 3:1**).

Since Christ is eternal in nature, His plans for us are also eternal in nature. The fatherhood of Christ to us is for both time and eternity. The capacity of Christ to father depends primarily on His nature. What can He not do if given the chance? We must not be deceived. He is actually inviting you to this living hope that brings nothing but real fulfillment and peace. He yearns to be your Father, for your own good and betterment; allow Him. Consider what will be your fate if you meet Him at the judgment bar without Him as your dad? Too bad! Make Him your Lord and not this world. Life independent of Him is the most counter-productive resolve any person could make, from the eternal perspective. The Lord Jesus Christ is the everlasting Father, who ever lived to minister to you all the fatherhood responsibilities to the perfect letter.

# CHAPTER EIGHT
# THE PRINCE OF PEACE

*'The only source of true peace in this life and beyond is Christ Jesus'*

OSMOND

## CONCEPT OF PEACE

Peace is a word desired by all, who may be rational and reasonable. Well-meaning people everywhere tend to pursue peace. There are many world bodies intended to establish peace in the world, but are they really capable of establishing the peace they are set up for? Do we really have the peace we so much desire for in our personal lives? Is it something attainable or it is illusory?

We want to now look at what peace is about, why the Lord Jesus is the acclaimed Prince of Peace, and how one could have this Prince of Peace establishing His peace in one's life.

From the Webster's New Students Dictionary, the word peace carries with it the following ideas: '

- State of tranquillity or quiet

- Freedom from civil disturbance or foreign war

- State of security or order within a community protected by law

- Freedom from disquieting or oppressive thoughts or emotions

- Harmony in personal relations

- Agreement between combatants or governments to end hostility.'

From the above, certain concepts are clear, out of which we may attempt to define peace. **Peace may then be defined as the state of tranquillity, security and orderliness that exists within an individual, between individuals, within a community or between nations.**

This peace we are talking about can be in the overt form (made open or manifested to be seen). The peace could be covert (hidden within the person). Whatever the case maybe, it influences the person's attitude, judgment, response and reactions towards himself or herself, other people and circumstances. This state of peace may depend on the environment or not. Someone may have peace, although the environment may be chaotic. In the pages of the Bible (Acts 7:54-60, Hebrew 11:35-40) and also in history books about the earlier church we find believers in Christ who were singing praises to the Lord as they were stoned to death, thrown to lions or even burning at the stakes. Today in all the poverty, disease, general societal retrogression, etc., some people still experience the peace of God that passes human understanding. Conversely you might find a business executive committing or with suicidal inclinations or embezzlement in the midst of plenty. We could also find a supposed man or woman of God abusing the spouse or stealing church funds in spite of all the truth they preach. Some people have spouses all right but still find cause into spousal infidelity. There are male adults raping minor girls and even infants despite the numerous female adults who might be ready for a relationship of a sort, etc., etc. So you see the peace does not necessarily depend on the circumstances.

We are looking at what goes on within an individual (intra-individual). The thought patterns, emotions, physical feelings, imaginations, etc., are the things we are discussing now. Whether they are things we could write home about; whether they promote tranquillity, security or orderliness and fair development for the person himself or herself, other people or the community as a whole. If the thoughts, the emotions, and every other thing that go on within the person do not satisfy these goals, then we say that the person has no peace. If what goes on within a person promote chaos, violence, hostility, rape, inferiority or superiority complexes, greed, inordinate sexual inclinations, bribery, suicide, theft and robbery, all manner of corruption, revengeful, envy, witchcraft, voodoo, fear, secret fraternities, drugs, etc., then the person has no peace. If **an individual is engaged**

**in the works of the flesh, then that individual is not at peace with himself or herself** (Gal 5: 19-21).

From the individual level, let us go to between individuals (inter-individual). Between people, peace is established or exists only when the partners involved have peace within themselves. **If there is no peace within them as individuals, then surely there will be no peace between them as a group of people.** The person could appear as a friend or even a blood relation, it does not matter. You will only realize in a matter of time that certain attitudes of this person towards you are not for your good. That is why you may trust someone as a friend or a confidant, but the person will later display some selfishness and turn may break your trust. It could even be your spouse, blood relations, church brethren, 'workmates,' 'bosom friends,' etc. It is just that such persons do not have peace within themselves. They may be aware of it or not. Let us take for instance; someone envies you for something you have gotten for yourself; not admiration but proper envy. This person will definitely fight against any thing, which could promote you if there is even the slightest chance.

Peace in a community or nation involves the non-violent, orderly situation in a community. We should find things moving on as predetermined by their constitution, if democratic, or by whichever code of order that is determined by the governing body in control. Thus the situation is as predetermined to be. It is individuals who make up communities and nations. People who are responsible for the decision-making for communities and countries are these same individuals we are discussing. The same non-peace situation within them definitely affects their decisions for their communities. No wonder we could find a lot of nations at war within themselves or with others.

We witness selfish, arrogant, greedy and oppressive leaders who plunge nations into poverty, civil war, and all the chaotic situations around us in this world today. Some go to the extent of even contracting wars with other nations. To go down to fathom out the real basis and motive behind this senseless massacre of people, you will discover, that it is nothing but raw, selfish, inordinate personal ambitions we call achievement. Sometimes these wars are just the settlement of old scores. Look at the political turmoil going on around us, in developing nations in particular. The real fact of the matter is that these people are simply deficient of peace within themselves.

There are seven major areas of human inclinations I want us to consider which actually determine whether or not someone has peace. For any normal rational individual, the following must be tangibly experienced for peace to be within the person:

- <u>Loss of spiritual touch</u>. God is the source of all life (John 1:4). Every other being created by God, when <u>connected</u> to God possess a sense of peace that flows from this God of peace. God is declared in the scriptures as the Lord of peace (2 Thess 3:16). Every person who is separated from God spiritually, deep down within the person there is a feeling of no peace and joy. People are alienated from God through wicked works (Ephesians 4:18). Thus if you do not have Jesus as your Lord and Savior (to be connected to God), then there is a spiritual vacuum that accounts for this lack of peace.

- Self-worth and confidence. People are not at peace when **proper** self confidence and self-worth are lacking. Self-confidence also affects personal vision and drive for life generally. This also affects the very means by which people achieve their goals in life. Imagine someone has superiority complex, what do you think may be the person's attitude towards other people. People with superiority complex tend to be oppressive and arrogant. A classic example could be the nazis, or any racist. Those with inferiority complex could be timid, hostile, critical, envious and often aggressive towards those they feel are superior to them. Proper, biblically balanced self-concept affects the very way by which one sees life.

- Purchasing Power of basic needs and sometimes luxurious wants is another issue. When one is not able to afford things he/she needs or desires, then frustration sets in and the person is not at peace.

- Self control. People lack peace when they are not able to bring their desires and emotions under control. Anger, sorrow, suicidal

78

tendencies, inordinate sexual passions, alcoholism, drugs, depression, etc. must be 'yoked' and brought under control. A person who is not able to control any desire or tendency to do evil or engage in any vice is not at peace with himself or herself. Any rational person will not feel at peace even when executing that vice. All energies and resources must be channeled towards biblically and socially adjusted ends for the betterment of oneself and humankind.

- <u>Sense of achievement and recognition.</u> Peace is lacking if a person feels not accepted or loved. There is instability when a person feels he or she has achieved nothing in life. A basic question like what have I lived in this world for, keeps nagging at the person's sense of worth. There is lack of peace when the proper mark or target for achievement, from the biblical point of view, is not first understood and secondly, attained.

- <u>Value system orientation.</u> There is instability in a person when that individual has developed a value system, which is not based on truth. Truth is enduring. The truth sets free (John 4:32). True liberty is established on truth. Truth is the foundation for freedom, peace and development. Therefore if a person is operating on a value system that is not based on the truth, this very person will then not have the desired peace. The person may not be able to specifically pinpoint the real problem, but this is the reality. The value system of this person is made up of the principles and ideas the person has internalized as a personal code of life. A proper value system is based on biblical principles, discipline and respect for human rights. A proper value system is having God's perspective on issues of life

- Sense of security. Peace is absent when an individual feels insecure. This could be financial, social, spiritual, etc. insecurity. A lot of people feel insecure, even at the point of death as well. Thus such persons may die not in peace. Lack of hopefulness (Eph 2:12) and general sense of goodwill towards life is also a demonstration of lack of peace.

## JESUS THE PRINCE OF PEACE

The Bible declares Jesus to be the Prince of Peace, and in fact He is our peace (Ephesians 2:14). This means that the Lord Jesus Christ is the sole custodian, controller, giver, sustainer, and the very personal embodiment of whatever is called peace. The kingdom of Christ is called the kingdom of peace (Rom 14:17). The Lord Jesus has a distinctive peace He offers **which cannot be substituted with anything in this world**, so declares the Bible. He says in John 14:27, *'Peace I leave with you, **my peace I give unto you: not as the world giveth, give I unto you**. Let not your heart be troubled, neither let it be afraid.'*

He is the real satisfier of life. He uniquely grants peace to all who humbly come to Him and desire for His peace. He is the bread of life. The Bible says in John 6:33,35, *'For the bread of God is He that cometh down from heaven and giveth life unto the world.... I am the Bread of Life: he that cometh to me shall never hunger; and he that believeth on me shall never thirst.'* He imparts peace to people who come to Him; and they shall never hunger nor thirst. This is because they become satisfied with life. In Him is life; he gives this life to every area of human endeavor we find ourselves. As we explore farther about this gift of God, one would realize that the peace of Christ Jesus permeates the spirit, soul and the body of an individual. It is not an academic theology but a real tangible life experience.

The peace of Christ is unique in every sense of the word. This is because it cannot be gotten from any other source. His peace is for now and eternity; thus as we live in this world and also in the consciousness hereafter. Revelation 21:3-5 reads, *'And I heard a great voice out of heaven saying, Behold, the tabernacle of God is with men, He will dwell with them, and they shall be His people, and God Himself shall be with them, and be their God. And God shall wipe away all tears from their eyes; and there shall be no more death, neither sorrow, nor crying, neither shall there be any more pain: for the former things are passed away. And He that sat on the throne said, Behold, I make all things new. And He said unto me, Write: for these words are true and faithful.'* **As we**

**submit to His principles of life, we receive and have peace within ourselves.**

Peace with God is the basis and foundation for peace within a person. The Bible says in Ephesians 2:13-18, that Jesus Christ is our peace. It is Christ who reconciles humanity to God; and this is what salvation is all about. As we become born again, we are reconciled back to God through Christ. This imparts into us a divinely sourced peace within our spirit and soul, filling the spiritual vacuum that gave us the inexplicable restlessness when one has not yielded to Jesus. This also gives unto the saved in Christ a sense of security one cannot explain in human terms but to simply acknowledge it to be part of you. This peace comes through only Christ Jesus. The peace is nourished as the individual continually depend on and live by the principles of Christ (Matt 11:28-30). It does not depend on anything earthly, not money, sex, personal goals achieved, etc. It is peace imparted to the spirit or soul of a person by the life-giving Holy Spirit.

As the Prince of Peace, Jesus Christ gives us hope for life. We are talking about the consciousness that all is not lost; but that there is a supreme God who is or could be your Father who really cares. With Him, no situation is hopeless. Christ in you is the hope of glory (Col 1:27). This sense of hope gives to one the inner strength to move on, and that all is well. This is hope which wells up right into eternity. This lively hope imparts into the believer a general sense of goodwill towards life and others.

If we consider the various aspects of the human life mentioned above, the Lord Jesus Christ satisfies all these to the fullness. He grants peace to all who come to God through Him. The Bible says in Colossians 2:10, *'And ye are complete in Him, who is the head of all principality and power.'*

The Lord Jesus Christ is able to save completely, those who come to God through Him, reconciling the person to God. As this reconciliation is complete, there is peace between the person and God; hence this person receives the peace of God.

Proper self-worth and confidence necessary for life depends on what a person knows and has. The Lord Jesus Christ on your side makes you the majority. You are more than a conqueror <u>through Christ</u> who loved you and died for you. Your knowledge of what Christ has done for you and is ready to support you in doing makes all the difference. He is our hope and confidence in this world.

The Lord Jesus Christ possesses the power to change your situation around, because He is the Creator. He gives us the power to make wealth. By His divine biblical principles for life we have the light that gives us the understanding and wisdom for a prosperous life. He is capable of establishing and protecting the work of our hands, so that in all things we could find life worth living on the planet earth.

The power of Jesus Christ as imparted to our spirit man at salvation, wise teaching in the scriptures, the support and empowerment of His Spirit makes us able to exercise self-control (2 Tim 1:7). He enlightens our mental faculties for us to have sound mind, and to understand heavenly wisdom and the essence of righteousness. As we yield to Christ to become new creatures in Him, we have peace and self-control, because it will then be Christ who is at the helm of affairs of our life.

When God approves you, dear reader, what is man? If God through Christ accepts me and loves me, human rejection should be nothing to me. The world will love their own, and hate the people of Christ (John 15:19, 2 Tim 3:12). As you submit whole-heartedly to Christ, your colleagues and relatives may not accept you, but cheer up because the Lord is on your side. Because things are so difficult for you today, people are rejecting you; you may even appear queer before them. Beloved reader, **rejoice for your Redeemer lives**.

It is very satisfying to achieve a dream of life. When you submit to Christ you will grow to acknowledge that whatever you could do in life is through the power and the wisdom of Christ (Deut 8:13-18). He is then to take all the glory.

The value system of the realm outside Christ is so porous and empty to the extent that people see material gains as a measure of one's life achievement **(Lk 12:15)**. No wonder human beings are not at peace with themselves and their fellow men. People pierce themselves with many sorrows for such gains that are of no eternal value. That is why some people cheat, kill other people for ritual or occult murders, join secret societies, steal, embezzle state funds, lie, libel others, live adulterous lives, racially discriminate, etc. All these are with a basic motive of having material wealth and the satisfaction of their selfish egos. Such people are destitute of peace (**1 Tim 6:9,10**). The value system of the world thus stimulates a wild–goose chase for things that are of no eternal value (**Mark 8:36,37**). Do not get me wrong in concluding that wealth, good job, etc., is evil. They are not ends in themselves, but rather they are comforts on earth that should rather aid us in expressing the love and wisdom of our Creator to one another.

The Lord's wisdom and order for life saves one from such woes and worries that have plunge the world into all sorts of anxieties, worries and uncertainties. As we follow the Lord Jesus Christ, He gives us peace through value-system re-orientation. He then ushers us into the reality of the eternal value system, which is able to make one wise in the real sense of the word. This is the value system, which is able to set one free (**John 8:32**) from unnecessary worries, depressions and the like.

Jesus Christ is the LORD, who is ever present with those who trust in Him. The presence of the Lord Jesus Christ gives the believer an ever-assuring sense and feeling of security. In the scriptures we find in many places assurances from the Lord of His continuing presence with His people. Primarily His presence is to protect, guide and direct their lives, if they offer Him the chance (Matt 28:20, Isaiah 41:10). Oh! What peace! Jesus is able to make His peace that passes all human understanding settle your heart and mind, when you earnestly seek Him for it (Phil 4:6,7).

This is the ALL-in-ALL gift of God. You cannot afford to let go of Him. Your peace in life for the now and ever more depends on Him and Him alone. He came to give life in abundance (John 10:10). It is time this very abundant life in Christ becomes a living reality in your life (John 4:14; 6:35). In fact, He desires you have His peace; this is the Prince of Peace (Matt 11:28).

## THE GIFT AS GIVER OF GIFTS

This gift of God called Jesus Christ Himself is also a giver of gifts. Thus Jesus as gift gives gifts to people to help them lead more fulfilling lives. This is just wonderful. The Lord Jesus Christ gives special abilities to people who come to Him. There are two basic kinds of gifts that Jesus gives to people who come to Him. Every other gift from the Lord is a derivative from these two.

Jesus gives the gift of salvation to us, through which we recieve His Spirit, called the Holy Spirit (Holy Ghost), given to help the person yield to Christ so as to become all that God wants the person to be. He is also given to aid the Christian to do all that God desires him or her to do (John 15:5). He is the Comforter Jesus entrusted His followers onto for guidance, preservation and edification. He empowers for service (of all kinds), praise, worship, holiness, understanding, remembrance, guidance, etc. The Bible says He is the Spirit of the Lord, counsel, wisdom, understanding, knowledge, might, and the fear of the Lord (Isaiah 11:2-5). Through the Spirit of Christ, Jesus blesses those who surrender to Him with all that pertains to life and godliness (2 Pet 1:2,3).

This same Spirit of Christ gives special supernatural abilities and grace (charisma) to people, called the gifts of the Spirit (1 Cor 12-14, Rom 12:4-8). The giving of the Holy Spirit by Christ to His people continues today. The Holy Spirit giving spiritual gifts to believers also continues till now. The ministries of the Lord and His Spirit, including His baptism, would go extinct when the five-fold leadership ministries also go extinct (**Acts 2:16-18, 32-33,38,39,Eph 4:10-16, 1 Cor 12-14, Rom 12:4-8**).

Unfortunately, some out of ignorance or probable envy, for apparent non-manifestation of the gifts in themselves, denounce these supernatural gifts of the Spirit outright. Others also denounce these gifts because of excesses some exhibits as they operate these gifts, probably out of bad training or pride. Others also look at these gifts with suspicion, because they suspect the operators might be using occult powers instead of the Holy Spirit. Yet still, others also just do not want to have anything to do with it, because of the fear of the unknown supernatural, or may think it's a bit into witchcraft or something. Some claim that in these modern times the baptism and the gifts of the Holy Ghost are completely out of place. This is because they feel that with all the sophistication of knowledge, technology and scientific methods of solving any kind of problem, the divine supernatural is out of place. Some also think they just simply do not want such things in their life, ministry or church, because the Bible contains everything they need today.

Alas, but in the apostolic days, the apostles through whom the New Testament was written were around, as well as the Old Testament canonized scriptures, but these gifts of the Spirit were in full-scale operation. Despite probable problems these gifts might pose, there is always increase whenever and wherever they are in proper operation (Pro 14:4).

In all this the Lord Jesus will never leave His people in the dark. The Scripture above, without prejudice, makes it clear that the gifts are still in operation today for the profit of all. The Lord is wise enough to give such gifts to the church, for the profit of all, in this dispensation of grace.

Secondly, He gives human beings as gifts to His body, called the church. These gifts are: apostles, prophets, evangelists, pastors and teachers (Eph 4:10-16). These are specific functional responsibilities the Lord Jesus bestows on certain individuals. They have the **awesome** responsibility of: perfecting the children of God to the maturity level of Jesus Christ himself (Eph 4:12,**13**). Secondly, they have to train believers to be <u>functionally equipped</u> and involved in the work of the ministry (Eph 4:12,16). Lastly, the leaders ought to build up the church in terms of increase in knowledge (quality) and also in number (Eph 4:14-16). They are accountable to their Lord who appointed them <u>primarily</u>, and secondly to their flock.

This is Jesus Christ the Prince of Peace. As one yields to Him, He makes you discover the true meaning and essence of what we mean by the word peace.

# CHAPTER NINE
# HIS OPERATIONAL
# CODE: THE ZEAL OF JEHOVAH

*'It is the Lord's intense, passionate, and unwavering interest to make sure that He uses all things at His disposal to accomplish His purposes and plans about you, as you keep trusting in Him.'*

OSMOND.

## THE ZEAL OF JEHOVAH

As the Lord of Host gives this gift, the gift has His own way of operating in the life of the receiver. With all the characteristics of the gift outlined in the above chapters, the recipient can really benefit from the gift if he/she really understands how He works.

In Isaiah 9:6,7 we read, *'...of the increase of His government and peace there shall be no end, upon the throne of David, and upon his kingdom, to order it, and to establish it with judgment and with justice from henceforth even for ever. **The zeal of the LORD of hosts will perform this.**'* From the scripture, the performance will come from the zeal of the Lord of hosts. So for anything at all we should understand what this zeal of the Lord of hosts is.

From the Webster's New Students Dictionary, zeal is defined as, 'eagerness and ardent interest in the pursuit of something: fervor.' Zeal infers energetic and unflagging pursuit of an aim or devotion to a cause.

From this definition, these few ideas are clear, that zeal:

- Is a deep passionate desire to get hold at something

- Is an intense interest to get something done

- Is a stubborn desire to get something done at all costs

- Is using all the resources one has to make sure an aim or goal is achieved.

Summarizing, zeal then means an intense, stubborn desire, interest or passion driving one to make sure all available resources are used to pursue an aim.

To relate this to our subject, the zeal of the Lord may then mean the intense, passionate, unwavering interest of the Lord of host to see to it that He uses all things at His disposal to accomplish His pursuits. Remember we are talking about the Master of the entire universe; the visible and the invisible. The title 'Lord of hosts' depicts JEHOVAH as the man of war, the victorious Commander of the ever-conquering army, the Lord who fights for His people.

Beloved reader, pause and look at this proposition about God carefully. Remember that God is infinite in all His characteristics and attributes. Thus the capacity and potency of His zeal to do anything is also infinite. Think about the Creator, who made and possesses everything and controls everything, has all power and wisdom, and has all skill and knowledge. He is just unstoppable in any pursuit of His. Absolutely nothing can stop Him from accomplishing any purpose of His.

The devil (a creature whom God uses, sometimes, to accomplish His purposes) cannot stop Him. Angels could not stop Him. Neither could demons, nor man, nor beast, nor the environment (physical or spiritual), nor any circumstance can stop God if He desires to do anything. We find the Lord using the devil to teach Paul about his limitations (2 Cor 12:7,8). We see similar usage of the devil by God in the torment king Saul went through when he rebelled against the Lord (1 Sam 16:14,15; 19:9).

When the scriptures say that the zeal of the Lord of Hosts will perform something, that particular thing is bound to come to pass at the very specific time God has scheduled it to take place. This is because it will be carried out with such might, effort, passion, skill, authority, military precision, discipline, and resources, that it shall surely be accomplished as at when He God desires. For sure it will be devoid of all slothfulness or laziness and shoddiness.

## OPERATING WITH THE ZEAL OF JEHOVAH

To operate with the zeal of the Lord of Host talks about these basic ideas:

- The operation is carried out according to Jehovah's working principles;

- The work is done in the most skillful and perfect way into a flawless and an enduring finish;

- The work is done in the power, strength, speed and vigor with which the Commander-in-Chief of the whole universe works.

- There is bound to be victory and fruitfulness

- The operation is what the gift is supposed to effect in your life.

Operating with the zeal of the Lord of Host cannot be possible if whatever is to be done is not going to fulfill His ultimate purpose and plan. Whatever Christ is to do in your life will in the long run give glory to God and fulfill His plans. As He directs and leads, there is bound to be only one thing; which is victory and victory alone. God will never invest in something, which will not ultimately bring honor to Him. If Christ, the gift of God, is allowed to do something in your life, then beloved your life is bound to shine forth and bring glory to Him and nothing else.

God never does anything that may violate His own nature and operational principles. This means that whatever He does will have to conform to His moral or holy standards. This involves the motive, and the methods. It also implies that God is not a respecter of persons. The Bible says in Acts 10:34, 35, *'Then Peter opened his mouth, and said, **Of a truth I perceive that God is not a respecter of persons** (Acts 10:34): But in every nation he that feareth Him and worked righteousness, is accepted with Him.'* It does not matter your background, the power of the Lord, through Christ is available to all, everywhere, who are ready to fear Him and to go by His principles of holiness and righteousness. God therefore works when humans are ready to do things His way.

Some people just want to have their own way in everything, but apparently run to God when they are in difficulty. In the work of the ministry, some ministers also go their own way by relegating the Lord to the background. That is why the testimony of the church is not strong in our communities today. Churches may be reduced to mere social clubs, destitute of the power, knowledge, and the operational agenda of the Lord today. If the leaders of our churches do not sit up and reconsider the Lord and how He the Lord works, things will take a different turn. Where His zeal is not doing the work, but we resort to mere human worldly wisdom and strategies, we end up with minimal heavenward results. In other words we grow people who are clothed with church jargons but are worldlier than they were before they came into the church. Our personal human ideas and methods can never achieve anything of eternal value (John 15:5). You may have a hall or chapel full of people but…Beloved, heaven backs us, and the might of the Lord is with us to achieve the results for Him when we do things His way.

The zeal of the Lord executes agenda in excellence. Jehovah is the God of excellence (Job 37:23, **Is 28:29**, Is 12:5). Whatever He sets His hand to do is done to a perfect finish, to a finish that is enduring and has no better alternative.

He knows the end from the beginning; he determines the seasons and the times; He sets one up and put down the other; He alone possesses all wisdom. He is more than capable to fashion things in the most effective way to achieve the best results from whichever perspective you may want to look at it. You and I must be hopeful and desire the most effective and best results for all our endeavors. We then need to embrace and receive into our bosoms the gift of God called Jesus Christ, which is far able to help us achieve **the results we actually need.**

The zeal of God carries with it the employment of the fullness of the very power, might, fervency and steadfastness of the LORD God Himself to execute His purposes. The very reason is that He cannot afford to put His reputation in the mud. An inability on His part to perform, if at all there could be one, makes Him a liar (a child of the devil then (John 8:44)). For not being faithful, etc., in fact, would have undermined His very essence of being and personality. God cannot therefore come into a situation for it not to be turned into the better.

As Christ comes in, He comes with all the might of the highest heaven; to make sure things go such as would declare His glory.

With Christ we are more than conquerors. Christ with you makes you the majority. Jesus Christ with you makes you the winner. Jesus is what makes the difference of significance, which is in fact in every realm of existence and endeavor. Jesus conquered death and He is alive forever more, and He has the keys of hell and of death (Rev 1:18). The Bible says that to His name JESUS every knee shall bow; whether in heaven, on the earth or under the earth, not only now but also in the world that is to come. All hail the power in the blessed Name of Jesus. The Bible says that, as many as shall call on the Name of the Lord shall be saved (Acts 2:21).

Just think about such a Name pregnant with such awesome power to set humans free. Jesus, when operating in our lives, is our victory. In the pages of church history books, we find such demeaning stories of some people who called themselves Christians and <u>were flatly defeated in a war they called crusades</u>. One thing must be clear, that **the God of the Bible <u>can never lose</u> in any battle, and will therefore not lead anyone to also lose**. Who can fight against Him (Isaiah 42:13,14, 43:13)? Who? He is the Master of all masters, King of all kings, and the Ruler of all rulers. He is far above all thrones, dominions, principalities and powers in every realm. The Bible says, in Ephesians 1:19-21, *'And what is the exceeding greatness of His power to us ward who believe, according to the working of His mighty power, Which He wrought* *in Christ, when He raised Him from the dead, and set Him at His own right hand in the heavenly places, **Far above all principality, and power, and might, and dominion, and every name that is named, <u>not only in this world, but also in that which is to come</u>.***'

For one to operate one's life with the zeal of the Lord means that you have submitted your life to the Lordship of Christ Jesus our Lord. This submission is to the extent that He leads you and empowers you to be more than a conqueror. Practically, your affair becomes His; and He fights for you. As He sees to your daily affairs of life, you are then under His direct care and control, and He backs you up with all that He is made of. Of course you are then entering and encountering divine provision and empowerment to prevail in this life and the hereafter.

The fight then becomes His fight. His name will then be at stake for your sake. Abundant supply of leadership, direction, resources, protection, favor, etc., I mean blessedness. Think about it.

We really must not miss this golden opportunity for any worldly arrogance. God wants us to have all this for ourselves and for His glory. Your life must not be the same again. God richly bless you.

# CHAPTER TEN
# THE INCREASE

*'He will bless them that fear the LORD, both small and great. The LORD shall increase you more and more, you and your children.'*

*'Anyone clinging to Him and submitting to His Lordship will experience limitless blessings and favor.'*

OSMOND

<u>Increase</u>, by the Webster's New Students Dictionary, carries with it the following ideas:

- To become greater in size, number, value, or power

- To multiply by the production of young

- Addition or enlargement in size, extent or quantity

- Something added to original stock by enlargement or growth

The first point appears to swallow the rest of them. Thus to receive an <u>increase in one's life involves the reception of an input to become greater in size, number, value, or power.</u>

So first there will be an input into your life, secondly this input will have an impact in your life, which results in your becoming greater in **value, power, number or size**. To become greater means that you will become better than you used to be.

The **value of a person** has to do with his/her relative worth, importance, usefulness, or esteem. It involves your personal honor; how wide your circle of influence is. How indispensable you are, is what we are talking about. It involves the extent to which people use you as a role model, how the public sees you, etc. In fact, it may appear that we are only concerned with, just the physical spheres of life, but no. Some people are so well known in the spirit-realm and their impact so great that even demons could testify about it. The Bible records two incidences in which Paul was identified as a threat to the kingdom of darkness. In Acts 19:15, the encounter of the seven sons of Sceva with the demoniac is one account. Secondly, in Acts 16:16-18, the encounter with the young girl who was a soothsayer, all testify about the impact of Paul's activities in the devil's camp.

Beloved the spiritual worth of a person is far fetching because its impact follows into eternity. It could be by way of evangelizing people into the kingdom of Christ. It can also be through an intensive and extensive prayer effort to destabilize the activities of the evil one. It can also be a consistent exposition of the Word of God to build up people in the faith. Whichever way you may want to look at it, the dividends are more powerful and it is into eternity when we invest in the souls of individuals.

We could also see the worth of the person in the physical, academic, social, political and business circles in terms of how much influence the person has in these areas. The respect the person commands, the level of authority of the person in his/her endeavors.

To increase in value has to do with the level of influence of the person in any of these areas. It also involves becoming greater, better, stronger and much more than before.

It could be physical or spiritual, but the fact is that the individual has grown in that particular field of activity. Someone could start as a mere beginner-teacher at an elementary school in an obscure rural setting, which may not even be on any map, but could end up as a lecturer in a prestigious university over time. One could start as a lay-preacher in an obscure place, but could end up with a 'mega' church ministry complex with TV and radio broadcasts.

To increase in **power** involves the growth in your capacity to get things done, because power has to do with getting things done. To get things done requires certain ingredients. Thus these ingredients constitute power, in the sense that, with them you could get things done. These are: wealth, knowledge, wisdom, skill, strength, health, authority and resources, etc. All of these are the components of power to get things done. Every one of them is crucial and essential for performance in any endeavor.

Therefore to increase also means, the **growth in capacity to get things done or your ability to increase your performance** in anything you are doing. Thus to be able to do things well, better and more of it is referred to as increase.

We see increase also as the swelling of numbers in anything under consideration. For example, one could start with one shop but would end up with a chain of stores. Someone may begin trading with a meager capital but it could grow up into billions. Another may be a minister who starts with a congregation of just his family, and later the member's number could swell up to thousands.

Here care is taken that the increase is considered only in the positive sense, not for example, beginning with monogamy and getting on into polygamy. We are not talking about moving on from pilfering into full time drug peddling and armed robbery. Neither are we talking about changing from multiple girl-friends to being filmed for pornography. The idea of increasing in number in a sense also means growing in size. These words are sometimes used interchangeably to stand for the same thing. Therefore the general idea one gets from the word increase has to do with growth in quality, quantity, usefulness, power, influence, etc.

## THE INCREASE OF GOD

The golden text, Isaiah 9:7, the Bible says that, *'Of the **increase of His government** and peace there shall be no end, upon the throne of David and upon his kingdom, to order it, and to establish it with judgment and with justice from henceforth even forever. The zeal of the Lord of host will perform this.'*

Here the Bible is talking about the increase of God's control over the situation, and the peace He thus provides will know no bounds if He really is in control over our lives. God is the One who is capable of blessing people infinitely; blessing without measure; blessing with everlasting impact; blessing that abounds into eternity.

There are many pages in the Bible, my dear reader, in which God speaks of His increase. The increase of God has to do with Jehovah God Himself who is to cause things to simply work in your favor. We are talking, about the situation where things could be adverse, frustrating, belittling, and apparently of no hope at all. When the divine hand of the most high God, the Creator of the heavens and the earth, by whose permission and power we live and move and have our being, begin to move over the turbulent waters of your situation, things become skewed towards your victory. It takes Jesus, for the breakthrough that is enduring and could stand for a comparatively longer time.

Impossible situations smile at us. It's not by military might, or is it by intellectual and academic power, but by the Spirit of the Lord; the mountains shall be made low and the valleys shall be filled. When this gift called Jesus Christ is operating in your life, my friend, it is then the ruling of the highest court in the total universe that determines the winner (Dan 7: 9). When someone satisfies His operative conditions set up above, and comes under the 'increase of the Lord,' power changes hands in the person's favor.

Not only does He cause your door of breakthrough to be opened to you, but also He causes the door to widen; He increases the opportunities for expansion beyond all that we could even imagine. His grace and power are able to cause you to become all that you could possibly become in Him and through Him (2 Cor 9:8).

The Bible says in Psalm 115:12-15, '*The Lord hath been mindful of us: He will bless us, He will bless the house of Israel; He will bless the house of Aaron. He will bless them that fear the LORD, both small and great. **The LORD shall increase you more and more**, you and your children.*'

When the Lord promised Abraham that He was going to increase the number of His seed. Little did Abraham know that truly, God will increase his seed, and that he cannot count his posterity, which include all who would come to God through Christ Jesus. At that time Abraham had no child. Interestingly, the nature of God's increase is able to transform him from a childless 'gray-haired' pilgrim to the father of many nations whose posterity is in continual increase till we are ushered into eternity. With the increase of God, Joseph, the Hebrew slave boy became one of the most intelligent and powerful rulers in a foreign land. Joseph's management skills saved the then world from the danger of severe famine and hunger. By the increase of the Lord Jesus, David, the shepherd boy became the greatest king in the history of Israel whose throne exists even today, spiritually, and continues forever.

Beloved this is how God could increase YOU through Jesus Christ, His gift. If He has done it for Joseph, David, Abraham, etc., He could do it for you. He says that He is not partial but that in any land people who reverenced God and lived righteously are accepted (Acts 10: 34,35). The Bible says that God knows the thoughts that He thinks about you; thoughts not of evil but of good that He may bless you and give you an expected end. He is still the same God. He does not change (Heb 13: 8). If you would adhere to this gift God has purposed for you with all seriousness that it takes, this very day forward, your life will never be the same again. Because of HIS great love for you, it is His fervent desire to bless you, and to empower you to prevail in life; so that your influence can have a lasting impact in your generation.

Do not think it is late for you by virtue of your age. There are many examples in the scriptures of old people whose life received divine intervention, through their faith, and they had a big laugh and a testimony at their old age. We also find others who were in apparently and utterly  hopeless situations. We have examples such as Sarah (Gen 21:1-5), Elizabeth (Lk 1:36), Rahab (Josh 6: 21-25), Shadrach, Meshach and Abednego (Dan 3:1-**30**). We are not forgetting the widow of Zarephath (1 Kings 17: 8-16), the woman who was twisted (Lk 13:10-13), the disciples (Lk 8:22-24), Peter (Lk 5: 4-8), etc. In fact, the list could go on forever. I think we also need divine intervention as well in our ministry, marriage, business, childbearing and upbringing, career building, etc. Sincerely speaking, you and I need God. Human strategies and experiences have their limit, and they do fail us. If we would be sincere, just look around us, the confusions, moral degradation, wars, hunger, disease, financial pitfalls, etc., are all proofs of this. Dear reader, we need God for every day of our lives. Through His gift called Jesus Christ, God is blessing and intervening in the lives of others, why not us.

## THE LIMIT TO THIS INCREASE

The increase of God has no bounds. The bounds may depend, primarily, on your faith and dependence on God; what you could envision, your compliance with the working principles of God.

The Bible says in the book of Malachi 3: 10, *'Bring ye all the tithes into the storehouse, that there may be meat in mine house, and prove me now herewith, saith the LORD of Host, if I will not open you the windows* *of heaven, and pour you out a blessing, **that there shall not be room enough to receive it.**'*

God is here calling forth for a bet if you wish, for someone to dare God. God is calling for a human being to test out the power of God to bless that individual, and two: the extent to which the blessing could go. It is time we take God really serious and faithfully check out God on this very challenge He has put before us.

Without doubt, with no compromise, let me state categorically that God possesses power to bless a person. In fact, the Bible says that it is God who gives us power to make wealth (Deut 8: 18). The ability, knowledge, and skill to generate wealth by any person, come from God. Look at something very carefully now: He has every resource in the universe, both spiritual and physical at His command. The earth is the Lord's and the fullness thereof. The Bible says that all things were made by Him and for Him, and for His own good pleasure were they made. Thus He can command things to come your way as He wishes and desires; no one could question Him on anything He does. Truly then the power for us to have the very things he has made, which is His, for ourselves, comes from Him, because they are for Him and at His command.

Therefore if anyone is truly wealthy, the person should be thankful and not arrogant. As He desires or has predestined you have the wealth,

He causes you to come by the necessary wisdom, knowledge, skill, opportunity, urge, grace, etc., to be able to acquire the wealth.

Secondly, God is saying that He could bless you infinitely; thus without bounds so that even after your death, your posterity will be enjoying the fruit of this blessing. Look, my dear beloved reader, if the Almighty God Himself is throwing this challenge to us, we better believe Him and go for it. This is because <u>He can truly bless us exceedingly abundantly far above all that we could possibly imagine or even dream of. This is because if He is not able to perform, if we meet the conditions, that makes Him a liar and unfaithful; and thus do not deserve to be worshipped. Therefore this puts God's reputation on the line.</u>

The unlimited God has power to bless a person to a limitless level. Do not make any mistake about this. It is simply detrimental to ourselves if we do so. We need to yield, at all cost, to Him in order to have His favor and blessings.

Some people just limit what Jesus could do as just the salvation of one's soul. But beloved, Jesus is calling us to things far beyond this; although that is the gate point to all the other blessings God has for us. The Lord calls us to share his life with us and we share ours with Him. This is just wonderful. It is one of the most powerful revelations in the Holy Scriptures.

Just look at it in Revelation 3:20, *'Behold, I stand at the door, if any man hear my voice, and open the door, **I** will come in to him, **and will sup with him, and he with me.'*** The mutual eating together in this text indicates that Jesus is calling us to share what he has with us and we are to share whatever we have with Him. This call is in the light of a loving friendship and fellowship to individuals or a group of individuals we could call church. Jesus desires to share our woes, failures, joy and triumphs with us (1 Pet 5:7). On the other hand He wants us to share all that He has with us. Just look at these: His authority (Lk 10: 19, Eph 1:19-2:6, Rev 3:21), as a Son of God (1 John 3:1, John 1:12) and as Heir of God (Rom 8:17, Gal 3:29, Gal 4:7). We are not forgetting Him as the coming Judge (1 Cor 6:2,3), His place of abode (John 14:1-4), etc.

Do we really know what this gift of God could do for us? Beloved, please pause for a brief moment and ponder, truly ponder, about the extent to which you are experiencing this very Jesus we are discussing in your very personal life. To what extent is He Lord over your life? May be you are going through tough times, or in your case things are apparently just fine. In all this, we should not be ignorant of the love of God and what really Christ Jesus desires for us.

Could we just pray. Examine your very life. Are you really on course? Are your dreams shattered? Are you in total confusion? Are you in a marital fiasco? What about your children, are they wayward? Does everything you touch fail somehow? Is your work gone bankrupt?

Have you accepted the confusion around you as one of those things, but inwardly you are continually hurting? The arms of Christ Jesus are wide open for you. Be very sincere to yourself and the Lord. Pray about this right now. Seek counsel quickly from the Lord. Do not give up yet.

## ULTIMATE BLESSEDNESS

God is eternal. His plans for people He calls are also eternal. So far almost all the things we have discussed are limited to the physical life as we are living on earth. The plans of God concerning YOU go beyond this world into the next world and thence into eternity. This is because we are not created by God to just live on this very planet earth and just die off after a little while. The existence of a person goes beyond this very world.

The human being is essentially a spirit who has a soul and lives in a body (1 Thess 5:23). The spirit is the center of God-consciousness; with it we have communication with God, who is a Spirit. With our spirit we contact the spirit-world. The soul of a person is the center of self-consciousness. With the soul we possess the sense of being oneself. The soul has three faculties namely: the mind, the will and emotions. The mind is the reasoning and thinking center. With the mind decisions are made. The will is capacity to choose between things; it is the power of choice. And the emotion is the capacity to feel. With our emotions then we are able to feel and express this feeling, whether pleasant or otherwise. The body is the center of physical-consciousness. With the body we are conscious of our physical environment, and are able to interact with it.

Thus the spirit and soul are non-physical aspects of an individual. The soul and spirit of a person are joined to the body by the silver cord. After physical death, when the silver cord is cut (Eccl 12:6), these two as one entity, return to the maker who is God (Gen 3:19, Eccl 12:7). The essence of this return is for judgment for the things done when given the permission to stay on this earth in this earthen body (2 Cor 5:10, Heb 9:27, Eccl 12:13,14). This judgment will place one into eternal damnation or into eternal blessings in the presence of the Lord. This judgment will be based on only God's standard, which is just, holy and true, without partiality or respecter of persons (Matt 25:31-46, Rom 14:11,12).

This is the plan of God. The human being is created and put on the planet earth to express God's image in him, and to have dominion over the things God has made (Gen 1:26,27). After death, you are to account to the One who gave you the permission to stay here. If you are found to be guilty, eternally you are damned. If you are found justified, eternally you are blessed (2 Thess 1:7-10, Rev 20: 10-15,21:1-8).

To then talk about the ultimate blessedness, beloved, we really mean three things. This involves being in the position where we receive the blessings of God in this physical life. Secondly, you go through the judgment justified. Lastly, you eternally rejoice in the holy Presence of the Lord Jesus Christ. I mean eternally rejoice! This is the plan of God for you, which nothing should stop you from attaining. Thus we are not limiting ourselves to just the things we could have in this life alone, dearly beloved. It should not be our thinking that getting wealth just for today is what matters. Reconsider and do not neglect the weighty issues of eternity. The bible says that we are of all people the most miserable and wretched if our mindset is living just for today (1Cor 15:19). <u>We must have eternal perspective of things</u>.

The Word of God categorically rules out evolution and reincarnation. These are affronts, from the western and orient worlds respectively, against the knowledge of God. The undercurrent to these ideas is atheism; thus total denial of God. Some people are atheist by their very way of life; they deny God completely in their heart but not in words lest the society see them as blasphemers (Psalm 14:1,2). These weird ideas seek to cause individuals not to recognize and retain God at all in their thoughts. To believe in evolution simply means that you do not have any Creator; hence you are not accountable to any one of your deeds after physical death. Evolution denies the original sin and the sinful nature of the human being which made Christ who is God come down as a human being to die in our place for us to be saved. Therefore the whole issue of a person needing salvation and Jesus as Savior of mankind if believed are reduced to rubbish. Evolution makes nonsense of the fact of God, His judgment and His plans for human beings. Reincarnation is quite similar to evolution in many respects, but it significantly denies completely that a person is given the chance to live on this planet once and that after death judgment (Heb 9:27).

Ironically, God has imbibed intrinsically within every person that He God does exist (Rom 1:19). The denial of His existence is purely then put forward by arrogant people who do not want to come to the Light, the Lord Jesus Christ, and as a challenge to Truth (John 3:19-21). They do not want to submit to God or be accountable to Him, out of pride. They will be laughing at the wrong side of their mouths. These thoughts are demonic from the pit of hell, calculated to deceive and enslave individuals to eternal damnation. Thus professing themselves to be wise, they are actually being fooled (Rom 1:21-23). The major advocates of these thoughts or the leaders of the movements are hard-core occultists and Satanist.

To be sincere to you, if any person will humbly appeal to his/her inner senses of the very existence of God, the person will know that God is. Do not be arrogant today, laugh this issue off and weep eternally in the lake of fire prepared for the devil and his followers (Rev 20:11-15, 2 Thess 1:8, Mark 9:43-48, Matt 25:41). Beloved, be warned and be wise. Remember God does not want you to go through this; God loves you (John 3:16).

It is God's wish that you are eternally blessed with everlasting life. Jesus says, *'I came that you might have life and have it more abundantly!'* Have and go for only the ultimate dearly beloved, and no mediocre things you call 'I have broken through'. Be eternally minded. We are talking about being blessed now and forever more, the ultimate blessing.

# CHAPTER ELEVEN
# THE PERSONAL RESOLVE

*'May your decision and resolve have value today and in eternity'*

OSMOND

## APPRECIATING THE GIFT

With all the things we have discussed so far: about God, and about His gift for humanity called Jesus Christ; one could make some meaningful deductions.

These deductions are that God does really exist. This treatise advocates that this very God is, in fact, unique in the real sense of the word. This God has infinite love for man to the point that He cannot look down on the plight of mortal man, but to move a step forward for our sake to sacrifice His own Son, Jesus Christ for us. Whosoever believes in Him will not perish but have everlasting life (John 3:16).

A person without Christ Jesus, according to the scripture just quoted, is perishing and therefore needs a savior. Man had fallen in sin; and had fallen short of the glory and standards of Jehovah God (Rom

3:23). By one person (Adam), sin and the fallen nature passed on to all humanity. Thus through one man sin and its consequence, which is death, passed on to all human beings, but through Christ we are made alive (1 Cor 15:21,22).

The fall of man got man's tripartite nature corrupted. The spirit of man became corrupted from serving and worshipping the living God to the worship of the creature (man, animals, plants, demons) instead of the Creator who is blessed forever. Idolatry is then the degradation of the spirit of man.

The fall of man corrupted our flesh. Human Beings then had the tendency to be involved in sexual perversion of all its forms. No wonder we could even have some ministers of the gospel who are sexual scandals today. Some even go ahead to conduct weddings for couples who apparently do not belong to the body of Christ, by wicked works, as married couples. Some church groups have trails of disgraceful and shameful acts such sexual indecency, even with minors, by their ministers. Reprobate minds, and abominations upon abomination, workers and ministers of the devil for sure are what we have today (Rom 1:21-27). Pornography in books, films, software and the net, in fashion, in ads, is the order of humanity today. Sexual immorality is the degradation of our flesh to the level of animal propensity; where we longer feel ashamed of illicit sex; just as animals do.

Thirdly, the fall of man corrupted our souls through inordinate passions, imaginations and emotions. Arrogance, wild outbursts of anger, murder, bribery, rape, embezzlement of corporate funds by few, robbery, ritual murders, etc., is a proof. In fact the list could go on and on.

Human beings then became cut off from the Lord God through sin (Gen 3:8, Isaiah 59:1,2). Human beings then by their own effort could not get back to God. This is  because there is nothing in the contaminated individual and the whole accursed earth that could meet the holy and just standards of God (Gen 3:17-19,Isaiah 64:6). The justice of God demands penalty for every sin committed. Therefore in sin, the human being stands in condemnation, and under the wrath and judgment of almighty God (Rom 1:18, John 3:36).

God then, in love, had to find a sacrifice for Himself that could meet His own standards. So that by that sacrifice, God could be appeased (Rev 19:13-**15**) and man could once again go back to God (the wages of sin is death, Rom 3:23). This is to give us the opportunity to have the blessings of God in this world and into eternity as well. Thus we could be reconciled unto God once again. This sacrifice is God Himself who came as a human to die in the place of humans in the person of Jesus Christ. What a deep love for us? God demonstrated His love for us in that while we were yet sinners Christ died for us (Rom 5:6-8).

When a person then believes in this sacrifice of Christ, we become saved from sin and its effects, become reconciled to God once again as children of God, have God's favor, etc. In fact, there is salvation in no name but Christ Jesus (Acts 4:12). In His name, every knee shall bow, not only now but also in the world that is to come (Phil 2:10). Thus through Jesus Christ we receive all that God has for humanity. He is the bridge between God and human beings. He declared thus, '*I am the way, the truth and the life*, **no man** *can go the Father but by me.*'(John 14:6).

Think about this very statement. The definite article qualifying these three paramount issues of life: the **way** for an individual to tread, the **truth** we must realize, and the very **life** for a person to possess. We need Him to be saved. Jesus Christ! He thundered, '*I am the resurrection and life, any man who believes in me though he were dead yet shall he live again.*' Jesus declares that He is the bread of life, the very satisfier of life. He says, '*All power is given unto me in heaven and in earth*'(Matt 28:18). This is Jesus Christ, the Prince of Life Himself. He is able to save or deliver to the uttermost those who come to God through Him (Heb 7:25). Beloved reader, we need Jesus!

The human being through sin, and the effects of sin had his or her capacities and potential **marred** from **optimum** performance in all spheres of human endeavor. Thus after the fall of man, it has become very difficult for him/her to be able to exercise all the faculties he/she was created with to the maximum; the glory is gone. This is also made

117

worse by the influence of demonic powers, which had invaded our planet, and subtly wrestled out authority and power from man.

The devil, the archenemy of God and his angels exercise authority over humanity until Christ came on the scene. The Bible calls the devil the adversary of humanity. He opposes everything good for man from God. He has been opposing man, so that man out of frustration may curse, insult and ridicule all that we call God. He is working 24 hours to make sure man forgets entirely about our Creator. Rather he desires we give glory to him, ourselves, or worse still degrade ourselves to the worship of things God has given us to enjoy on this planet (Rom 1:18-32). These evil powers and their human agents, not only do they seek to divert people from God through vain philosophies but also influence people adversely; thus making life tough, and empty.

Apart from reconciling us with God by salvation in Christ as mentioned above, to be able to breakthrough these two major setbacks confronting humanity; we need Christ. The wisdom and the power to live on this planet and really prevail over these two in this very life are embodied in Jesus Christ. The bible says that HE is the very Wisdom and Power of Jehovah God (1 Cor 1:23,24). The bible says in Romans 5:6 that, *'For when we were yet **without strength**, in due time **Christ died for the ungodly.'**

Thus all ungodly people do not have the strength and the power to prevail in this life from God's perspective. If the ungodly will turn to Christ for strength, beloved, there is victory (Lk 10:19). Jesus Christ is

118

offered to us so that we could have access to God's power and wisdom to live successively in this world. We are talking about being saved, going through life as a child of God in holiness, enjoying God's blessings on earth, going through judgment unscathed, and eternally being with the Lord with laurels of faithfulness. Jesus Christ as the gift of God for us is given so that we, as we receive Him and go by His ways will be able to have all these successfully. He is able to **make all grace and all power abound towards** you to accomplish anything according to His will for His glory (2 Cor 9:8, Eph 1:16-19).

You will agree with me, dear reader, that any self-well-meaning person could not ignore this all-embracing gift of God. You need to appreciate this parcel of God for you. He is for you.

## THE NECESSARY CHOICE

Here is the multibillion-dollar question: what do I do with Jesus Christ. There is always this question before mortal man about this all-important choice concerning the offer God always makes to us. This happened to Pontius Pilate about two thousand years, whether to let go of Jesus or to reject and crucify the Lord of glory. Pilate had all the necessary evidence as a basis for accepting Christ but he rejected the king of glory for sake of the world (Lk 23:22-24, Mark 15:15).

Apostle Simon Peter had the same opportunity, and he rejected Jesus Christ three times, but thank God he humbly recovered and accepted Christ. Jesus accepted Peter and blessed him, Peter was lifted to the status of apostleship by the Lord's own appointment; and now his name is one of the foundations of the New Jerusalem (Rev 21:10-14).

Judas Iscariot had the same opportunity but blew it up with one of the most raw, bizarre and gruesome betrayals in the known history of this world.. Yea, he walked with Jesus, ate with him, heard Him preach and perform miracles but did that to the Lord of lords. Judas betrayed the Lord with that evil kiss.

The second robber on the cross knew better and he made the right choice, which I sincerely believe made him have eternal life. The evidence before him was just enough to convince him that the wisest thing to do is to humble himself and surrender to the Lord for mercy, pardon, and salvation. The Bible says that the Lord Jesus instantly lifted this person that same day to be with Him in paradise! What a glorious picture of our merciful Lord at work here. You could also have the same kind of lifting today!

All the people mentioned and many more had the same or similar opportunities to accept or reject the Lord as you have just now. The Bible says Jesus is the Light of the world that lighted the way of every man that came into this world (John 1:4-10). Judas, Peter, the thief, Pilate etc., are not with us now. You may have laughed at the decisions of these people about Christ. This is our day. This is our time and generation. What are you doing about this gift of God called Jesus Christ? This is a personal resolve and the most important decision one has to make. It is not just about just receiving Christ Jesus as Savior of your soul. It goes far beyond that. Jesus desires to be the Lord over your life for your own good.

Please, dear reader, it is my fervent prayer that you receive this gift of God and give the Lord Jesus Christ the chance in your life. Do not let the adversary (1 Pet 5:8) use the pride of life, the lust of the flesh, and the lust of the eye to deceive you. You may have received Jesus as your Savior a long time ago. **It is time you tangibly experience the living power and the very vibrancy of the life of Christ Jesus in your daily situations and circumstances.**

Many read about prayer but yet remain prayerless as ever, so do others who read about financial success but remain broke and bankrupt. The key to being lifted from lack to abundance, from sorrow to joy, from backwardness to blessings, etc., lie in the practical action you put to the knowledge you have received about these. In other words you benefit from this publication if you would take the knowledge you have received from it seriously and act upon it.

# EPILOGUE

Jesus Christ is Lord. He is inviting you and I every day of our lives to come unto Him, all of us who labor and are heavily laden and that He will give us rest to our souls. Jesus is the only lover of your soul. The Bible says that a nursing mother can deny and reject the suckling but He the Lord will never reject you nor forsake you. All humans could reject you but Jesus can never abandon you. He says that **all who come unto Him, He shall in no wise cast out.**

Jesus is the only **Lifter** of your head. Promotion is of the Lord; it does not come from the east nor does come from the west but it is of the Lord.

For the storms and fires of life, beloved, they shall surely come. The Lord has promised in Isaiah 43:1-3a, *'But now thus saith the LORD that created thee, O Jacob, and He that formed thee, O Israel, <u>Fear not: for I have redeemed thee, I have called thee by thy name; thou art mine. When thou passest through the waters, I will be with thee; and through the rivers, they shall not overflow thee: when thou walkest through the fire, thou shalt not be burned; neither shall the flame kindle upon thee. For I am the LORD thy God...</u>'*

What a promise from such a faithful God? What else do you want in life? Look at Psalm 94:14, *'For the LORD will not cast off His people, neither will he forsake His inheritance.'* He will never leave you until He has quite finished with you.

Beloved, in conclusion, let me say that may the God whose desire is that you may encounter His blessings through His Gift Jesus, from His riches in mercy, might and wisdom bless you in all things. May you experience this God in growing proportions and on daily basis. May God bless you.

# About the Author

Pastor Osmond Owusu is a Ghanaian by physical birth and a Christian by spiritual birth. He is married to Felicia Owusu and have four kids: Theresa, Frederick, Philip and Gideon.

The author holds a Bachelors degree in Mathematics and Science and has also graduated from a school of Pastoral Studies. He has been teaching high school math and science. He has been active in Christian ministry, and has served in different capacities in the Assemblies of God (A/G) church at different locations in Ghana, and also in University Campus Fellowships. He has been a regular youth conference speaker at regional and district levels of Assembly of God, Central Region, Ghana. He has been a patron to several campus Christian youth fellowships.

Pastor Osmond is currently in the US with his dear wife Felicia and their children. The author is the Pastor in charge of Christian Education at Rockwall First Assembly of God Church, Texas. He also teaches at the Greenville High School Texas.

For ordering and comments about this book, speaking engagements, seminars, and revivals, the author can be reached by email: osmondsco@yahoo.com or www.osmondowusu.org